THE EPIC OF QAYAQ

He has Lost his Paddle

Syollie Amituk

THE EPIC OF QAYAQ
THE LONGEST STORY EVER TOLD BY MY PEOPLE

Lela Kiana Oman

Edited by
PRISCILLA TYLER & MAREE BROOKS

Preface by
ANN CHANDONNET

CARLETON UNIVERSITY PRESS
CARLETON UNIVERSITY ART GALLERY
(OTTAWA)

UNIVERSITY OF WASHINGTON PRESS
(SEATTLE)

Printed and bound in Canada
Published simultaneously in the United States by the University of Washington Press, P.O. Box 50096, Seattle, WA 98145-5096

CANADIAN CATALOGUING IN PUBLICATION DATA

Oman, Lela Kiana, 1915-
    The epic of Qayaq : the longest story ever told by my people

ISBN 0-88629-267-0

    1. Inuit—Alaska—Folklore. 2. Legends—Alaska. I. Tyler, Priscilla II. Brooks, Maree III. Title.

E99.E7042 1995   398.22'0899971   C95-900224-3

LIBRARY OF CONGRESS CATALOGUING IN PUBLICATION DATA

Oman, Lela Kiana
    The epic of Qayaq : the longest story ever told by my people / Lela Kiana Oman ; edited by Priscilla Tyler & Maree Brooks ; preface by Ann Chandonnet.
    p.   cm.
    ISBN 0-295-97531-8
    1. Qayaq (Legendary character) 2. Inuit—Alaska—Folklore. 3. Legends—Alaska. I. Tyler, Priscilla. II. Brooks, Maree. III. Title.
E99.E70424 1995   95-51536
398.2'089'9710798—dc20
          CIP

Cover and interior design by Karen Temple
Front Cover: Zacharias Kunuk, *Drum Dancer* (1985)
Back Cover: Nutaraluk Iyaituk, *Dancing Woman* (undated)
From the Priscilla Tyler and Maree Brooks Collection of Inuit Art at Carleton University Art Gallery. Photos by Susan Close.

ACKNOWLEDGMENTS

Carleton University Press gratefully acknowledges the support extended to its publishing program by the Canada Council and the financial assistance of the Ontario Arts Council.

The Press would also like to thank the Department of Canadian Heritage, Government of Canada, and the Government of Ontario through the Ministry of Culture, Tourism and Recreation, for their assistance.

CONTENTS

PREFACE

Ann Chandonnet

FOR CENTURIES, INDIGENOUS PEOPLES OF ALASKA, Canada, Washington and Oregon have upheld the artful tradition of oral literature. These creations were handed down from one generation to another, under stringent protocols designed to keep intact their cultural significance.

The most substantial form of oral literature is the epic, which may take many days to relate. The shortest form is the riddle, a brief set of clues that requires an answer from the audience. Of intermediate length is the parable — a single instructive incident from "another time."

Other forms of oral literature include songs, recitations of lineages and rights, ritual greetings to visitors, ceremonies for distributing gifts, ceremonies for honoring the dead and ceremonies celebrating marriages or births.

Traditional Alaskan storytelling is a rich art, originally part of a brilliant universe of oral tradition that included shaman's songs, potlatch greeting songs, epithalamia, and much more.

Lela Kiana Oman's *Qayaqtuagaqniqtuq*, or *The Epic of Qayaq: The Longest Story Ever Told By My People*, is an Inupiaq Eskimo epic, told to her when Oman lived at the mining camp of Candle, Alaska. Her own account of how she first heard these stories and from whom is detailed in the introduction.

During the day, Oman worked as a cook in the Candle roadhouse. During the late evening, when the roadhouse was closed and her own five children were asleep, she wrote down these stories.

But earning a living as a cook, a social worker and bilingual teacher occupied Oman's time for many decades. It was not until 1992 that she spoke about the epic at the Eighth Inuit Studies Conference in Quebec.

The epic follows the adventures of Qayaq, a traveller who wanders by boat and on foot in northern Alaska and Canada and even makes an excursion among the Tlingit. Qayaq is the youngest of twelve brothers; the eleven older brothers have all left home on adventures, never to return. His mother assigns him a quest: "to save the human race from evil."

The epic includes the story of the Inupiat Adam and Eve, the story of a great flood and a tale that is a corollary to the Biblical tale of Jonah and the whale. To the Kwakiutl of Vancouver Island, it was Halibut who crawled out of the water, threw off his scales, tail and fins, and emerged as the first man. To the Haida, man crawled out of a clam shell at the northern tip of Haida Gwai (today known as the Queen Charlotte Islands). In Oman's version (in her "Preamble"), the first people are a man and wife who suddenly come to consciousness on a mountain peak. Food and game are plentiful, and many children are born to them. Years later they discover other people living on the other mountain of this limited world, and their children intermarry.

Oman feels the story originated in the area where her parents grew up — the riverine valleys of the Kobuk and Selawik. However, versions of this story are known to the Eskimos of Russia, Canada and Greenland as well, which indicate it is circumpolar in nature.

Oman's story is straightforward. It is perhaps a digest of the original epic, which could have taken as little as a week or as much as a month to tell. To grasp its full import, consider some of the traditions of the oral storyteller.

Although they are given full play in forms like songs, figurative devices such as metaphors and similes are rare in indigenous Alaskan stories. Iconography and symbolism are also rare, so that a seven-headed monster is a monster with seven heads — not a symbol of the seven deadly sins, as such a creature would be in Spenser's *The Faerie Queene.*

Eskimo stories often came with venues. Some would be told only on solemn and highly formal occasions. Some were told to children and grand-children on domestic occasions or at particular camps (sites of temporary nomadic residence), such as the ground squirrel stories told at spring's ground squirrel camps. Stories were never intended for secular public performance where persons who were not members of the tribe might be present.

Titillating details or clues are a frequent story-teller's device. For example, at the very outset of Qayaq's adventures, he kills a seal and hauls the head into his skin boat. Magically, the head of this dead mammal growls at him! This is a clue (both to Qayaq and the audience) that the head has unusual powers and may come in handy later on. Clues like this inject suspense.

Perhaps the most unusual aspect of Northwest stories is the theme of transformation. This is not the temporary transformation of princes into frogs or geese as in the tradition of the Brothers Grimm. It is a permanent ability to change shape. Bears take on the appearance of men and marry human brides. Sea otters imitate humans and precipitate boat accidents and drownings. Raven turns into a spruce needle, a human foetus and then a human grandson. Fish have their own "villages" and "hearths" beneath the water, can speak to humans and advise them. In Northwest tradition, the resemblances between human lifestyles and animal lifestyles are meant to show that animals are worthy of the same kind of respect from humans that humans give to one another.

Epics always take place in a "Story Time," that once upon a time when animals and people were closer in the great chain of being, could communicate and thus learn from one another more directly than through simple observation of "the other."

Northwest stories — like oral stories handed down throughout the world — are generally not for amusement alone. Usually they have an important social purpose. One purpose is to supply examples of what true heroes do. Heroes are almost always male and single, so that they may wander; they are not constrained to return to the village regularly with game to feed an extended family. Like the ancient Greek hero Ulysses, Northwest heroes typically undergo initiations of increasing severity, slay monsters, demonstrate strength and cunning, collect important tools / wealth / power / skills. They free the enslaved and punish hubris, arrogance, greed and cruelty.

Secondly, heroes also demonstrate how cleverness and sly tricks can, as in the British folktale of "The Little Tailor," compensate for lack of size and strength.

A third purpose is to demonstrate the importance of adhering strictly to tribal ethics such as respecting animals, fish, and other sources of food.

Stories may be whimsical such as "The tree that became a man" in Edward Keithahn's *Alaskan Igloo Tales*, but they tend toward the moral and the cautionary — just as do Mother Goose rhymes and the Brothers Grimm tales.

Common themes run through these stories: the lure of adventure / foreign territory; respect for tradition; revenge; conflicts of loyalty; the journey to maturity and judgement — often via a series of encounters with creatures that are not human; responsibility to the band / village / tribe rather than to the self; transformation (appearance vs. reality); courage; perserverence; ingenuity.

Among Northwest peoples, human existence is viewed as a series of tests and trials, of propitiations, of encounters with powerful chiefs / shamans and powerful supernatural forces.

Stories come in a variety of lengths. Shorter tales, like the story of how Raven's feathers became black, may take only a few minutes to recount. Such a tale could be told to relieve the tedium of a brief task, like fetching water.

The leisure necessary to telling an epic often came during the coldest days of winter, when paths were choked with snow, rivers with ice and even the game dug in.

Story time might also surface during evenings of a memorial ceremony (often performed a year after a death).

According to some sources, epics are told in a definite sequence that cannot be varied. Other sources say the storyteller may choose the sequence. The issue of order aside, a series of episodes is recounted during several evenings. No other story is begun until the epic has been heard to its completion.

Some sources say the storyteller may be interrupted by his audience, who may shout out corrections if he falters or mis-remembers. (This interesting notion makes storytelling a community effort, with the teller perhaps the person with the best voice or pronunciation — but not, perhaps the best memory.)

The custom of storytelling occurred among all Alaska's people. Charlie Joseph (1895-1986) of Sitka was raised in a traditional Tlingit settlement at Lituya Bay when only Tlingit was spoken there. He recalled, "In the evening, stories were told. I don't remember when we missed an evening of telling stories. It was like going to school today, when my grandfather told all the stories, the ancient stories [*tlaagu*] we remember throughout our lives" (*Haa Tuwunaagu Yis, for Healing Our Spirit,* Dauenhauer, p. 540).

Readers will notice that Oman's story sometimes loops back upon itself and repeats certain elements. If a hunter after a moose in thick brush loses his quarry, he circles back until he finds the trail again. Just so the storyteller circles back — especially if the story is epic in length, and being told on consecutive days. The storyteller's motive for circling is that he or she fears the listeners will be unable to take up the story's thread again without this aid. (Modern teachers employ this useful mnemonic device.)

The aim of bringing Oman's work to the world in a transcribed format has been to allow the reader to experience the epic fully — not to make it sound literary.

Some references to everyday objects and scenes in the text may remain suggestive but as undescribed as they were in the original. This is because the original audience for the *Epic of Qayaq* was a homogeneous group, and no description was necessary. As Bill Holm wrote in his Foreword to the Coast Salish tale *Eye of the Changer* (Alaska Northwest Publishing, 1984), "Words can build pictures and evoke sunsets and storms, but they can only hint at the lines of sleek canoes, the gnarl of a root, the sweeping branches of the cedar or the angle of the adz handle."

Like an actor, the storyteller employs dramatic pauses, differing tones of voice, dialect or accents and laughter. These techniques do not always survive on the page, so evocative adjectives and adverbs have occasionally been added in their place.

Northern peoples often use a pronoun (especially "he") where, to English speakers, a noun would be clearer. There may even be two "he's" in a sentence, each referring to a different antecedent. Nouns have been inserted in such confusing instances.

Northern peoples employ circumlocution when discussing beings or activities that embody spiritual power or luck in the hunt. A bear, for example, is too powerful to mention directly, so he might be referred to as "that big brown one." The indirect reference shows polite deference and avoids alarming a potential quarry. Where indirect reference could be unclear to a modern audience, a more direct reference or an appositive has been added.

Throughout, however, editing has been applied sparingly so as to preserve as much of the original's flavor as possible.

Readers who wish to compare the *Epic of Qayaq* with another Northern epic should seek out *K'etetaalkkaanee: The One Who Paddles Among the People and Animals: The Story of an Ancient Traveler* by Catherine Attla (Yukon Koyukuk School District and Alaska Native Language Centre, Fairbanks, 1990).

Like Qayaq, K'etetaalkkaanee is a young man who leaves his mother and undertakes a quest to pursue his dreams and gain spiritual power or "medicine." As he paddles all summer and walks all winter, this hero meets obstacles and overcomes dangers, witnesses the transformation of animals, establishes customs and illustrates wisdom.

Catherine Attla was born in 1927. She heard the story of K'etetaalkkaanee from her grandfather, Francis Olin, a medicine man of the Kokuyuk River. She recorded the story in Denaakk'e, the Koyukon Athabascan language. It was translated into English by Eliza Jones and published as the third in a series of stories Attla has preserved.

The closest analog to Oman's epic is *The Longest Story Ever Told: Qayaq: The Magical Man* by Ticasuk (Emily Ivanoff Brown). Published in a limited edition by Alaska Pacific University Press (Anchorage) in 1981, this book is not well known. In Brown's story, Qayaq has four brothers and an uncle. He is able to find the female temptress and killer of all four brothers, and takes revenge on her.

Brown first heard part of the legend from a Mrs. Auligi of Shaktoolik when she was seven, camping in the mountains of the Bering Seacoast. She heard other bits and pieces at boarding school in Salem, Oregon, and elsewhere. At 64, Brown became a student at the University of Alaska Fairbanks precisely to master those skills that would enable her to preserve this epic and other stories, and completed extensive research to find the "missing parts" of the story. According to Brown's version, Qayaq was born at Siilvik Lake, near Eschscholtz Bay, in the western Brooks Range. His parents' village was Selawik.

Comparing Oman's and Brown's versions on the Qayaq sequence is a fascinating exercise. In general, in Brown's, there is considerable concern for preparation before the quest and for the feeding of the extended family. In Oman's, the beauty of the landscape and pleasure in this beauty are themes returned to again and again.

To compare and contrast a specific episode, the episode of the giant bird, in Oman's scenario it is Qayaq himself in human form who discovers the bird's "Achilles' heel" and kills it. The powerful bird recalls the mythic roc in the "Sinbad the Sailor" episode of *The Arabian Nights,* and the too-ing and fro-ing over the tundra battlefield has the formal order of battles outside the walls of Troy.

In Brown's version, however, this mythic formality is absent. The giant white bird is, although outsize, familiar — a huge ptarmigan; and Qayaq defeats it by transforming himself into another creature colored for winter, an ermine. The ermine crawls beneath the snow cover, bites the bird's artery, and sucks blood from its leg until it faints. Then Qayaq assumes human shape again and cuts off the bird's head. The ends of the two versions are identical, but the means are quite different, with Oman emphasizing both the speed and distance the great bird can cover and Qayaq's persistence, and Brown emphasizing stealth, the ermine's ability to tunnel beneath snow, and the use of magic amulets that aid transformation.

Oman's "Preamble" bears a striking resemblance to another Northern story, the first section of *The Eyeshade People*, a lengthy Upper Kobuk Inupiaq narrative told by Robert (Nasruk) Cleveland of Shungnak. This story is one of twenty-four contained in *Unipchaanich Imagluktugmiut: Stories of the Black River People* (National Bilingual Materials Development Centre, University of Alaska, Anchorage, 1980). Robert Cleveland was born in 1884 along the Kobuk River. Cleveland's stories were recorded in 1965 — at a time when Cleveland himself felt his memory was not what it once had been. After Cleveland's death in 1973, Minnie Gray of Ambler, Cleveland's daughter, transcribed the stories, which were then translated by Ruth Ramoth-Sampson.

When Cleveland tells the story "At the Time of the Flood," he emphasizes its local relevance: "Actually, it is more than just a legend," he says. "It is about what happened in this area, the valley, during the great flood." To emphasize the point, he adds that he has himself seen remnants of the dwellings of the people of the flood high on the mountain sides —
just as Qayaq reports seeing remnants of their boats.

Storytellers like Oman, Attla, Brown, and Cleveland are stewards of culture. With no written language to preserve traditional Athabascan and Eskimo stories, their stewardship is invaluable. Unfortunately, however, as stories are handed down over successive generations, and as they are translated from their original language into others, some cultural details inevitably fall by the wayside, and the story may be condensed to a mere string of "he did this, he did that."

Language is the most complete embodiment of a culture, and a story without its original language is only a shadow of, or scrapbook of, the original.

Nevertheless, when so much of Northern indigenous cultures has been washed away in the flood of new influences of the last 250 years, one can only be thankful that dedicated individuals like Lela Kiana Oman have persevered in preserving what follows.

Without her patience and dedication, we would have nothing.

With her, we have this shining glimpse into an Inupiaq treasure chest.

Poet and journalist Ann Chandonnet is a 22-year resident of Alaska, contributing editor to Alaska *magazine, and author of the children's book,* Chief Stephen's Parky *(set in the Athabaskan village of Knik in 1898; Roberts Rineheart, 1993). She was a feature writer for* The Anchorage Times *for ten years, and now works as a freelance editor and book publicist. Her culinary history featuring many details about indigenous cuisine,* The Alaska Heritage Seafood Cookbook, *will be released later this year.*

INTRODUCTION

Priscilla Tyler & Maree Brooks

THIS EPIC DESCRIBES QAYAQ'S WANDERINGS BY KAYAK and on foot along four rivers, the Selawik, the Kobuk, the Noatak and the Yukon, as well as up along the Arctic Ocean to Barrow and over to Herschel Island in Canada; finally he makes a short excursion south to a Tlingit Indian village.

The epic reveals Qayaq as an adventure-loving wanderer who gradually assumes the role of doing good for people. He uses the supernatural powers his mother and father give to him to win in combat and overcome obstacles. He is also on the alert for contributions to the culture of his people, such as the copper-headed spear, and his last contribution, the birchbark canoe.

Qayaq lives with animals as well as human beings and on occasion transforms into an animal himself. In the epic he becomes a caribou, a weasel, a ptarmigan, a hawk, a mountain sheep and a fish.

That these tales must have been told for many thousands of years is indicated by truly ancient stories such as that of the Big Flood, and by textual details, such as the absence of dogs from the epic. In the Flood story, Tulugak, the Raven Man, saves the people from the rising waters by hurling his harpoon at a whirling clod of earth, which then expands, making the waters recede. In the comparable Biblical myth, Noah sends out a raven to find

land but the raven never returns to the ark. Lela says that raven came to Alaska to save her people. As to details which help to date this epic, dogs are mentioned in the "Preamble" but not in the epic itself. Dogs were introduced into Alaska about 1000 AD, so these stories are very, very old.

Episodes in this epic often resonate with other popular myths and Biblical passages. One instance is when Qayaq's brother sends word for Qayaq to come to Barrow to destroy the sea monster that is devouring young men there. This story is reminiscent of the story of Jonah and the Whale in the Old Testament. Seventeenth-century translators of the Bible used "whale" for the Hebrew word for "sea monster"; so this story echoes the Biblical myth very distinctly.

Greek myths also bear a resemblance to Eskimo mythology. The myth of Scylla and Charybdis in Homer's *Odyssey* presents a situation similar to one encountered by Qayaq on the Noatak River. In both myths the hero gets through the dangerous passageway in the water, and in this epic, Qayaq destroys the clashing cliffs and stills the water to allow *all* people safe passage on the Noatak River. This shows the benevolence and the power of Qayaq.

Another example of Eskimo mythology echoing Greek mythology is the killing of the one-footed stone bird by Qayaq. He strikes the bird with his stone knife in its one vulnerable spot, the ankle. In post-Homeric legend, Thetis attempts to make her son the infant Achilles immortal by dipping him in the River Styx. This story first appears in writing in

Publius Papinius Statius' epic poem, "Achilleid." Popular mythology has added that since Thetis held her baby by the heel, Achilles remained vulnerable in that one spot. This powerful image survives in everyday speech today. Later myth holds that Paris kills Achilles by thrusting his sword through his heel. Here is a striking similarity to Qayaq's method of killing the one-footed bird. How old any of these myths really are or where they really came from we do not know. But such echoes make it seem possible that these myths are related in origin.

Now we want to tell how Lela happened to write this epic. The roadhouse Lela Kiana Oman ran in the mid-1940's in the mining town of Candle, Alaska, was the meeting place of many Inupiat miners and travellers. Some of the men spent their evenings telling stories of Qayaq. Lela got the idea of sharing these stories with a larger audience. So after the men had told them, Lela sat down at a table and wrote in English the stories she had heard in Inupiaq. Lela recalls:

Aniviaq Kapiasruraq (Frieda Goodwin), a cousin of my father, and a gifted storyteller, sat at my side during some of the nights when I was writing. She contributed her memories of the Qayaq story she had heard many years earlier.

Her husband, Charlie Goodwin, was employed by the mining company at Candle for many years. Together they contributed much-needed happenings to Qayaq's travels while I was trying to piece together this story of *Qayaqtuagaqniqtuq*. I spent many pleasant hours listening to legends they knew. Charlie was a good hunter and ably cared for Frieda, who had much knowledge of fur sewing. While they lived in Kotzebue they told many stories on the radio and in the evenings were often called to give talks at the community hall, where they also told many stories.

Much of what I have written I heard from my father, Aqsiivaagruk Agsiataaq Kuugnaq, Jim Kiana. He was born about 1870. I have been told the story of his birth. His father, Kiana, dug into deep snow reaching the ground that was solidly frozen, way back away from people, among the thickets. Still, when a fire was built this was warm enough for the delivery. Here the baby and his mother, Asruguaraw, spent their four-day confinement. This snow hut was hastily put up for this occasion. Her mother, Anayuqauraq, attended the birth. She was my great-grand-mother and she was known to be a strong shaman.

Anayuqauraq, my great-grandmother, was the grand-daughter of the Umialik Qauqaq through his first son with his first wife, Atuan.

Qauqaq owned the whole Kobuk Valley and the Jade Mountain. He had five wives and four of his wives each had twelve children. He had much respect from others. He had been taken home by the white-bird mother and had been gone for five days. At the age of ten winters he was chosen by the mother up in the sky and was told that he was going to grow up to become an Umialik (Chief).

The white-bird mother up in the sky said, "Many that have the same blood from your veins will trod this whole world. You are a prince and you are my own son."

From the Kobuk Valley eastward to Canada and to Greenland many have said they had originated from the

Kobuk River. Umialiks of Barrow, Point Hope and Cape Prince of Wales have said that this Umialik Qauqaq was their true grandfather. As the Umialik, he had to be a spokesman of many village gatherings. At this time there was a huge *qazgi* (community hall) where people gathered to listen to tales, histories, news from outlying villages, and to learn from their seniors. To be a good listener was to be a survivor in many cases.

If the new religion had not intervened my father would have been a strong shaman to carry on the great powers of his ancestors. Still, he felt he was a very strong one spiritually. The dying sent for him to pray for them.

Loving us, his children, he entertained us the best way he knew how and left to us many legends that he knew. "Be careful and do not hurt the people that are around you. You are not just Eskimos — you are descendants of the people that were great."

To put us to sleep he told us stories. He did not see telling old stories as sin. He and the old people had seen much before the new Christianity came, and they could not completely forget it. If they had we would not have known their history, told entertainingly in story form — stories of people that could have disappeared into oblivion if they did not do their utmost to preserve them. "Work hard and be clean to be worthy of these people who are your ancestors": many times my father told us this.

Another source for these Qayaq stories was Nathaq Eviviq, Susie Kiana Lockhart. She was my father's younger sister. Susie claimed to have originated from space, along with a sister and a brother. In her search for a mother she had roamed the Earth among animals before she finally became a human being.

She was a gifted storyteller and she had many stories. She had absorbed much of the native stories which I have written in my books. In 1934 I stayed with her at Kotzebue. Many a night I fell asleep while listening to her stories.

George Avinuuluk Washington had brought his large family from Buckland to Candle while he worked for the mining company there. His oldest daughter was working for me at the roadhouse. She and I would go to their house to listen to stories after work. In the year 1947 I had made it known that I must write some legends and for this reason my visits to this family were sometimes nightly. Avinuuluk expected us and was ready with Qayaq episodes. One night he explained to me that his ancestors were from the Kobuk Valley and that one of his Eskimo names was the same as my father's. On account of this he called me "Panin" (my daughter). He looked upon these visits as a recognition of the relatives that had gone ahead of him.

His wife, Flora Kayuqtuq Thomas Washington was a daughter of Suuqii Thomas from Kingity, Cape Prince of Wales, a descendant of the great Chief Suuqii. Shortly after the Noorvik village was settled, Suuqii moved his family to this location. He wanted to be close to the doctors, schoolteachers and the new religion that was then dominating the area. They came with sled deer and were pretty spectacular as they arrived at Noorvik. As a little girl I remember seeing this beautiful family. They were well-dressed in fur garments, light in complexion, but short and stocky. After unloading their belongings the older boys helped their father take their sled deer to the tundra near by.

Flora became a good midwife and must have delivered

well over a hundred babies. In Candle, in 1947, she was listening to the tales her husband was telling, not only as a listener, but also to prompt him. She knew these stories, too.

Jim Quyliaq Hadley called me "*Uuyungun*" (niece). He said his parents originated from the people that lived on the Kobuk River and Selawik River. He was a distant cousin of my father's. He was a trapper and his small family had a nice camp at Snyder's some 18 miles above Candle on the Kiwalik River. This place he had built out of sod and his shelter saved some travellers who were caught in storms. He moved around with his good dog team. Sometimes he stayed in the roadhouse. Sometimes he came in just to get a cup of coffee and these times were precious to me. These were the times that I could listen to some legends. Some parts of the Qayaq story I obtained from him.

Lela left Candle in 1947 and the stories lay in a box for nearly 30 years. In 1975 she looked at them and wished to make a month-long tale out of the many pages of writing. During the shortest days of winter, when there was no hunting, it took a whole moon, from new moon to full moon (some 14 days),

for an Inupiat storyteller to tell of the wanderings of Qayaq. They were stories that had been told for millennia by Lela's ancestors, both as a record of actual events and as a history of her people.

Lela says: "Many tribes in Alaska feel that *Qayaqtuagaqniqtuq* (Forever-riding-a-kayak) is their own story. Claiming it as their very own, they say, 'It came from our river!' This man Qayaq had travelled much, he and his eleven brothers had done much to rid Alaska of evil in man and animal. Many Eskimo under four nations — Russia, the United States, Canada and Greenland — know this story." *

Lela goes on: "I feel that what I have written is an opening for someone to be encouraged to continue this work, so generations to come will know what our people were like at one time. Here, in my own selfishness, I could say that the story began from my own two rivers, Kobuk River and Selawik River. My father coming from the Kobuk River and my mother coming from the Selawik River."

Lela Kiana Oman, who was born in 1915 in the Kobuk Valley of Alaska and grew up there, was of

* Episodes of Qooqa in Greenland are similar to episodes of Qayaq in Alaska. At the Eighth Inuit Studies Conference in Quebec in 1992 Kirsten Thisted of the University of Greenland presented a paper on "Qooqa" (a hero with a name like "Qayaq"), a novel with an episodic structure like Lela Kiana Oman's *Epic of Qayaq*. *Qooqa* was written down by Greenlandic writer Ole Brandt (1918-1981). Thisted said, "Everybody knows Qooqa and the book may be the most well-known and most popular book in the whole of Greenlandic literature." She went on: "The first time it was broadcast on the radio in the early 1970s the cities as well as the small settlements were dead because everybody would sit inside listening, and afterwards episodes from the story would be retold orally." They were like the stories their forefathers told. *The Epic of Qayaq* and *Qooqa* tell many similar stories of their hero's adventures. In each there is a sea monster, a terrible storm at sea, the improvement of hunting methods, as well as supernatural happenings.

the first generation of her people to use the written language to preserve the oral tradition and she is of the last generation to know the oral traditions of her people. Lela has a great mastery of the written word, just as her ancestors had a great mastery of the spoken word. We think you will agree when you read what she has written.

We will now turn to some of our own insights into the *Epic of Qayaq* and how they relate to Eskimo life in both ancient and modern times. A recurrent theme in the epic is community and Qayaq's encounters with different kinds of community. Near the beginning of the epic, Qayaq leaves his parents at the mouth of the Selawik River, not too far from Kotzebue, an ancient trading centre. He lives for a time with a family of hawks, who appear to him as human beings. From them he gets an important tool, a double-bladed hatchet, which along with weapons from his father (the spear, the bow and arrow and the stone knife), and the copper-headed three-pronged spear (gained from his meeting with the fisherman who is also an otter), he brings along and uses often throughout his adventures. From his early experiences, Qayaq emerges prepared in both practical and supernatural ways to help people and to defend himself.

Later Qayaq visits a community of animals living as people and sees how they treat each other. Living among the mountain sheep is Qayaq's first experience of community. The mountain sheep-as-people live together in harmony, with everyone helping one another. It is a peaceful time for Qayaq.

Through the epic, as Qayaq visits communities of men and women who are not animals, there is only one community of humans who have a peaceful way of living together. Significantly, that one has a leader who is a kind old shaman. At one point he says, "My Shaman-ancestors were like me. They used their supernatural powers kindly and wisely. I am sure my path of peace was paved for me by them before I took powers from their souls." By contrast, three of the communities Qayaq visited had leaders who were cruel to the people in one way or another.

The first community of men and women that Qayaq visits is the Umialik's community. More is told about Umialik and his community than is told about any other person or community in the epic. Here Qayaq learns from his wife about the Big Flood and how the Raven Man saved his people. Also, Qayaq's wife, the Umialik's daughter, tells how her father (then a young man) came across a cave where the souls of the men, women and children who died in the Flood stayed on earth as the Living Dead in this cave on the Kobuk River. At death their souls were not taken to the place beyond the sky where they become living again because there were no birds during the time of the Flood to take them there. From time to time Umialik visited this cave. He got inspiration for his way of life from these souls. The importance of these stories is that Qayaq learns about the continuation of good and evil inherited from the ancestors.

For example, Tulugak, the Raven Man, was at first

reluctant to do anything to help his people during the Big Flood because he had so little faith in his ability to succeed. As a consequence, some of his descendants were shiftless and lazy. They carried on the uncertainty of self-worth inherited from their ancestor, Raven Man. In Umialik's case the inheritance of good or evil also comes into play throughout his life. The Umialik's grandmother is a lovely person and is very caring for her family. But she has a life of sorrow and becomes a whiny old woman because she had evil ancestors. The Umialik himself cannot overcome his inheritance from these same evil ancestors, and turns to bad ways over the course of life.

The direct inheritance of destiny in life is paralleled by the Eskimo belief in the immortal soul after death. Umialik's grandmother tells him: "When a loved one dies or is lost, he or she comes back in many different ways. Some are born as a baby and some are made known through animals or in dreams that they are around again." The theme of immortality recurs with each community Qayaq encounters.

The evil Umialik's community is also rich with insights into the Eskimo sense of good manners and ritual. We attended the Bering Straits Elders Conference in Nome, Alaska, in 1989. Several hundred Eskimos were in the conference hall together and it was very quiet. Drumming and dancing went on nightly for a week, but during meal times it was very quiet. People talked to one another with quiet voices.

In Umialik's community it must also have been quiet. Sometimes people communicate without words. They communicate with their eyes or with actions. There are three good examples of speaking with eyes only in the epic. Qayaq's wife loves each one of her girl helpers and "They understood this and returned her love, showing it in obedience and in their shining eyes, never, never, in words." Likewise, all the people in the community obeyed Umialik, "show[ing] him their love in their eyes, but never, never, never, in loving words." And after her father's treacherous efforts to kill Qayaq, his wife "looked at Qayaq with a question in her eyes, but Qayaq met her eyes with a smile and did not say a word. She understood his silent answer."

Sometimes people communicate with actions, taken without words but nonetheless eloquent. In Umialik's community their importance is clear. When Umialik grieves alone, face to the wall, after failing to kill Qayaq, the text runs: "Why was he grieving? No one would ask Umialik for they knew he would never be able to explain his hurt. No one would ever be so undignified as to openly discuss Umialik's feelings with anyone." When Umialik was seen "talking directly to Qayaq" the other boys went on into the mountains to hunt alone. They understood with not a "single word" being spoken that Umialik had chosen Qayaq, not one of them, to be his son-in-law. Similarly, there is a point in the epic where Qayaq's wife's girl helpers are whispering among themselves. She gives them a "swift glance," and they became quiet. She had "given them a silent order" — no words were needed. The Eskimos today seem to have quiet community meetings. Perhaps it is a trait handed down to them from their ancestors.

The Eskimos feel there is a strong spiritual bond between humanity and all of creation. After leaving his wife with her father, the evil Umialik, Qayaq goes into the mountains. He needs to get in touch with nature and lift his spirits. There he has an encounter with a flock of ptarmigans who appear to him as human beings, and an adventure among the caribou. Qayaq is invited by their leader to become one of them. He gains a new perspective on everything and learns that the only way to run without falling is by keeping his eyes on the distant horizon. After looking for the heights of space, Qayaq has a much stronger sense of nature, and of how wonderful and precarious an animal's life can be. Before coming down the mountains into the next community, Qayaq achieves peace with nature. By day "The sky was very blue and everywhere he looked spelled peace," and by night "Infinity showed few stars." Lela says the space beyond the earth is infinity. Gazing at infinity Qayaq becomes more conscious of his soul.

To approach the new community without being seen, Qayaq undergoes a series of transformations quite different from those in his earlier adventures.

This time, Qayaq's soul leaves his body and he travels as a little weasel to the village below, leaving his apparently lifeless body behind. Then he transforms again into a fluff of down. Finally he transforms and becomes a man again. These powers awe the community and Qayaq frees them from their three tyrannical leaders. But it is a strenuous encounter, for Qayaq must change from man-to-fluff of down-to-weasel once more in order to re-enter his body. The next morning his body is stiff and sore. It is very painful to the body to be left without a soul.*

When Qayaq returns to the community in human form, he finds an atmosphere very different from the quiet of the Umialik's community. Here people speak to each other and drum and dance and laugh. They act out stories that are being sung. But while celebrating their freedom from the three tyrannical leaders over four days (this is how long it takes for the soul to leave the body, the Eskimos believe) the community is nonetheless observant of the careful dinner ritual, refined manners and the death rites. Qayaq is witness to, and sometimes a participant in, all of these practices. The community feasts so the dead men's souls have food and drink and they dress three boys so their souls have clothes to wear. This is done to keep the immortal souls from coming back to haunt them. The three men were evil but it was this

* There is another transformation later in the epic, when Qayaq joins the Tlingit community. He becomes a hawk and is eaten by the Tlingit princess. Although he becomes a disembodied spirit and loses his flesh and bones, Qayaq can still think and eventually arises, phoenix-like, to marry the princess.

community's custom to honour the dead in this way.

In the third community Qayaq encounters, he undergoes a trial against village leaders which stretches over three days. But he spends the evenings with a little boy and his grandmother. In their home Qayaq feels free for the first time to talk about his brothers and parents. This grandmother is the only woman in the epic to have supernatural powers for good. Qayaq seems to give of himself more in this community both in his reaction to the helpful old woman and her cute grandson and later to the young lady, Nii-viq-siq, who is the only person in the epic other than Qayaq to have a name. (Umialik and Angatkuq are titles as Shaman is also.) Qayaq watches over Nii-viq-siq as a wolf and then as a kind and caring young man, but apparently never becomes her husband.

At the end of the epic, Qayaq goes home.* In Oman's epic Qayaq looks for the place at the head of the Selawik river where he had left his kayak so long ago. He finds it has crumbled with age. He needs a kayak to travel to the mouth of the Selawik River to his parents' home. He cannot make a new kayak because his had been made from sealskin and he was far from the sea. For the first time in the epic, Qayaq calls for help. He looks up to space and shouts to the universe: "I have overcome evil with good in my many travels…. My power came from something great. Or someone has helped me. If there is someone who has helped me, I need help now. There is a Greater Force than I know, I need help now." This time, a community of animals comes to Qayaq's aid. They make him a birchbark canoe, so he can get home.

We have pointed out some of the things that interest us. There are many more points of interest that we have not mentioned in this introduction. Those we leave for you, the reader, to find as you enjoy the ages-old *Epic of Qayaq*.

Priscilla Tyler
Professor Emeritus, Department
of English and Education
University of Missouri
Kansas City

Maree Brooks
Teacher, Librarian
Shawnee Mission
Public Schools,
Kansas

---

* In Emily Ivanoff Brown's book *The Longest Story Ever Told,* the hero Qayaq returns home, too. Some of the stories she collected from the people at White Mountain who believed their ancestors had originated from falcons. Her ending has Qayaq returning home where he "handled the old implements of his father and mother, and this touch transformed his sadness to gladness in his heart." Then he changes into a falcon and flies, "to the Koyukuk Valley, the land of the forest, where there was quiet and peace. He can be seen there yet, still in the form of a falcon, but ever ready to turn into a man again if he ever is needed to right a wrong or overcome evil."

The River at Netsiilik

Pitseolak Ashoona

PREAMBLE

Lela Kiana Oman

A man and his wife found themselves on top of a mountain. With them was a dog. Where they came from they did not know. There were all kinds of animals around them. To the east of this mountain was another mountain. The two mountains were connected by a narrow neck of land. And all around there was water, water as far as their eyes could see.

There were all kinds of good things to eat growing on the ground and it was easy for them to catch any kind of game they felt like eating.

Children were born to them and as their children grew, their land grew larger, too.

One day the father was walking alone along the east side of the Western Mountain. He happened to go farther than usual. On the other end of that narrow strip of land, he saw another man. He was so surprised there could be another man like himself. He walked toward the stranger smiling and that other man was smiling, too. When they were within speaking distance the father said, "So there are some other people on this earth!"

"I did not know there was such a man as I am on this earth, too," the father added. "I live on this mountain with my wife, my children, and our dog. Come with me and I shall show them to you. I am very glad that there are some people like we are."

The two men had the same language, but neither knew how they happened to be living separately on these two big mountains, one on the west and one on the east. This man from the west compared everything on the Eastern Mountain with his own at home and everything was the same. He visited them awhile and when

* *The word "Eskimo" has been used throughout this book to refer to the Arctic people of Alaska. From 1947, when the epic was written down, to the present time in Alaska, "Eskimo" has been used by the people to designate themselves. Lela's people, who speak Inupiaq and live on mainland Alaska, are called "Inupiat." Yupik-speaking people living on St. Lawrence Island and on the Kuskokwim Delta are called "Yupik."*

he started for home, he asked to take the father of this family home saying, "I want to show you my family, too, and I am so happy to know there are people like us. I want my children to know your children." So he took the man of the Eastern Mountain home with him.

From time to time, the families of the Western Mountain and the families of the Eastern Mountain visited each other. Finally, their children started taking each other as husbands and wives. Those on the Western Mountain did not want to be separated from their children; so they moved to the Eastern Mountain. Many years the two families lived together on the Eastern Mountain. Their children had their own children so they became many in number.

By this time, their land had grown so big that they could not see the water any more. As the land enlarged, the animals had more space to roam, so they started scattering. This made them hard to catch. So the people that started from these two families began to have a hard time getting enough food. To make matters worse, the ones who came from the west were getting short-tempered, and they began to practice shamanism. When they were not pleased, they killed off people by taking their souls, knowing a man cannot live without a soul.

This is why the West Wind is usually stormy. It is because the people from the West were temperamental and stormy natured. People from the East were always easy-going, peaceful and kind. That is why the East wind blows softly and warm, while the West wind is very often stormy.

Finally, each man took his family and moved away from this mountain and did his best to make a living for his family. This scattered people everywhere.

THE EPIC OF QAYAQ

THE LONGEST STORY

EVER TOLD BY MY PEOPLE

Lela Kiana Oman

The Hunters Capture Whales
with their Harpoons and Sealskin Floats

Joe Talirunili

This is the story of Qayaq as it was told to me by several different storytellers ...

At this time, the days were long and the nights were short. Summers were long and the winters were short.

In the lower valley of the Kobuk River lived two families beside a slough and two lakes that had no outlets. They were very strong and seemed to be well-off. One summer the children went off for a day of berry-picking. When they came home, they found their parents had been clubbed to death. Some giant, a killer, had come upon the two sets of parents and put an end to them. This frightened the children, even the grown children.

The children scattered. Some went inland to the East, some went toward the North and one man and wife went South to the mouth of the Selawik River. These two were very strong and hunted sea animals on the Selawik Lake. At this time Selawik Lake was very deep and was a playground for huge whales. The man and his wife would go out in their kayak and bring home a huge whale. They also made use of other animals of the mountains and tundra.

As time went on, the family increased. Many sons were born to the couple, but as soon as each one got old enough to hunt alone, he would go away on a hunting trip and never return. He would push off from the sand spit which shelters the mouth of the Selawik River and paddle his kayak up the river. That would be the last his family would ever see of him.

After the eleventh son had left home in this manner just like his older brothers, the father and mother felt they could not face losing their twelfth son, who was still just a baby. But the father knew it was likely that when this boy grew old enough to be a great hunter, he would also leave in a kayak and like the others never return. The father grieved over this. Once a son had left, he knew that he would never see him again. In his grief, he kept saying to himself, *"Qayaqtuagaqniqtuq"* (Forever-riding-a-kayak).

One day the mother was down by the river cutting fish to dry, while the baby, Qayaq, was sleeping in their huge sod home. The father climbed up on the strong roof. Standing above the open skylight, the father looked down and watched his son sleeping. In his mind he saw Qayaq leaving them in his kayak. What will become of him? What had happened to his other eleven sons? Each one always promised that he would return, but none had ever come back.

The father at this time thought to himself that he was going to know what happened to this one. From the skylight he shot at the sleeping baby with his bow and arrow. The baby Qayaq bounced away from the spot; in the spot where he had been lying the deadly arrow quivered without harming the child.

Once again, the father tried to kill his son. This time he was eating close to Qayaq, then a boy of about six winters. He tried to stab his son with the knife he was holding to cut his food. Although Qayaq was not facing his father, he quickly moved away from where his father sat. The father tried this a few more times but had to give up when he realized that he could not harm his gifted son.

Qayaq grew and became strong and quick in movement as his parents were. He was allowed to hunt on land and the large lake, but his father always forbade hunting along the river. Qayaq always wondered what would happen if he paddled against the current of the wide river. From time to time he sat on the pebbly beach and looked up toward the East quietly and longingly, wishing to explore. His parents recognized in him the desire to test

LELA   KIANA   OMAN

himself away from home that the eleven older brothers had shown before they left.

Both Qayaq's parents were very strong and quick in movement. They lived on food they caught with spear, knife, bow and arrow. On their two legs, they could run and overtake the swiftest animal running on four legs. They were fast swimmers, too, and caught much food from the big lake. The passing of many years seemed not to have any effect on them. They looked and felt as young as the day they took each other as husband and wife. Still, they knew Qayaq was their last child, and he was very dear to them.

The day came when they could not keep him from going. His mother made *akutuq* (Eskimo ice cream) for him to take along. She chewed on caribou fat to make *akutuq*. And his father rendered fat from a recently killed whale. For many hours the *akutuq* was stirred. Starting from a liquid state, the oil from the whale and the fat of the caribou were stirred together. As the mother stirred, the liquid became foamy and was enlarging. As it grew, it became white like snow. For the last ingredient, the mother gave herself a nose bleed. This blood was added to the growing bulk of the *akutuq*.

The mother said to Qayaq, "My dear son, it is not in my power to keep you with me. I have no supernatural powers for I am the daughter of the Eastern Mountain. With you will go peace, which is the makeup of my body. The blood I shed into this *akutuq* shall be your youth and your strength. I am sending you out into the unknown world that you might be able to save the human race from evil. My wind is a very kind wind; may the other winds be kind to you. Take a taste of this blood of mine when hopelessness seems to be overcoming you." She ladled the *akutuq*, now pink with her blood, into a leather pouch.

Qayaq put the pouch into his sealskin packsack. In his kayak were a spear, bow and arrows; a stone knife hung in a case from his belt.

The parents sadly followed him down to his skin kayak, and from the beach his father picked up three small pebbles. The father was a descendant of the Western Mountain. His mother was a descendant of the Eastern Mountain. Did not the people of the Western Mountain start the practice of shamanism? There were magical words he knew, and to protect his son he sang songs that had supernatural powers to save and to kill. His son could think of these songs in times of danger to protect himself.

The father said, "My son, you are a man like me. There is nothing I can give you from my body that is not already yours. However, I have a few magical words that I feel you should have." Pronouncing a word he picked up a little pebble and made Qayaq swallow it. Three pebbles he made Qayaq swallow. Each little pebble was given to him with a magical word. "If you think that you are breathing your last, you must remember the little pebbles — each and every one will be useful to you, at separate times.

"My other gift will be a song with power. When you sing it, it will become a rope, a rope with ability to kill or whip anything and make you strong. You will have to overcome the elements. Out there are people like us. Maybe you will need this supernatural power to protect them and yourself."

The father and mother wanted Qayaq to come back, and not to leave forever like the other eleven sons. All during his childhood, Qayaq heard his father lamenting, "*Qayaqtuagaqniqtuq*" (Forever-riding-a-kayak). Qayaq was told over and over again that his older brothers had left one by one in a kayak, against their parents' wishes, paddling up beyond the bend. Although each one had promised that he would come back again, none had ever returned.

In spite of his responsibility to care for his aging parents, Qayaq could not neglect what seemed to draw him to go beyond the great horizons. Chances were, he might find out what kept his brothers from coming back.

"If I come back, I will bring news of what has happened to them," Qayaq promised. Qayaq kept looking back at his parents as he paddled away from them. They became little dots on the pebbly beach of Sauniqtuq.

While still close to the mouth of the Selawik river, he caught a seal. He severed the head and put it in his kayak. Although it should be dead, it was growling at him. This was strange, just a head growling at him. He talked to it and told it to be calm. It was going to be a help in some way.

When he reached the first bend of the river he noticed what seemed to be a dwelling. He went ashore to see who could be living there. No one greeted him as he beached his kayak. He hid the growling seal head under his arm inside his parka. He noticed a large sod house and around it were racks on which human skins were drying. A woman came out of the large sod house.

The woman invited him into her sod house, acting like she was glad to see another human being. The seal head under his arm growled, but Qayaq did not heed the warning and followed the beautiful woman into her dwelling. When he passed the door he heard the creak it made; this made him look back, only to see the door was swinging shut. It was a trap. When the woman grabbed for him, he shoved the growling seal head at her and made a leap for the door. He made his escape and ran down to his kayak. He paddled hard up against the current. As he did so he heard screams amidst the growls of the seal. He knew that the woman had no chance of survival.

QAYAQ ASSOCIATES WITH BIRDS AND ANIMALS AND A MAN WHO TRANSFORMS INTO AN ANIMAL

Man and Seal
Rupee Natsiapik

Qayaq paddled and paddled.

Just a river bend away from the woman, he noticed a man fishing. He had a three-pronged spear poised in the air to strike, and was looking intently into the water. Qayaq wanted the spear. The spear had gleaming copper tips, and in the sun it shone brightly. The man holding the spear was so absorbed in what he was doing that he did not notice Qayaq. Qayaq paddled backwards and got out of the man's view. He beached his kayak and dove into the water. As he did so, he turned into a good-sized pike and, as a fish, swam in the water toward the man. He swam very slowly and went directly to the spot where the man stood. The man saw him in the water within striking distance.

"Ah! I am going to eat, ah mm-mm!" the fisherman mumbled to himself. Qayaq gave him a big stare, and the man did likewise in a split second before he struck. Then with all his might he sent the copper tipped spear into the fish. Qayaq felt it in his shoulders. With the help of his strong tail he gave a big twist. He heard a snap of the spear as it broke. He felt the pain of the spear points in his shoulders and neck, but he was still conscious and knew that he was free. He swam back to his kayak and changed himself to a human. He went through a painful time while pulling the spear from his shoulders. After he pulled it out, he healed his wound by taking some saliva out of his mouth and spreading a thin film of it over the bleeding wound.

Then Qayaq got into his kayak and paddled around the bend again. When he saw the man he had robbed of the copper spear, he went ashore. The man was busy tending his fire. He was mumbling to himself as if he regretted something very much. When he saw Qayaq he invited him to share his food. The man had very white and sharp teeth when he smiled. Fish were cooking over the fire. The sight and smell of them made Qayaq very hungry. When the fish were done, the fisherman with big teeth was going to lay them down between them when he took a good look at Qayaq.

"Looks like I have seen that bridge over the nose before," the fisherman said, indicating Qayaq's bridge between his eyes which was very high. "You, as a fish, took my spear!" This accusation startled Qayaq.

"How dare you insult me!" With these words Qayaq reached for his knife, that was hanging on his belt. The man with big teeth jumped up and ran into the thicket close by. Before he reached it he had started to change shape and he ran on four legs! He looked back and Qayaq saw his furry face. He was no longer a man but an otter.

"You shall never catch anything but with your teeth." Qayaq bellowed these words after the furry fisherman. To this day otters must use their teeth to catch their food.

Qayaq put out the fire and picked up the fish and walked to his kayak. Now he had a three-pronged spear to add to what he had brought from his home — an ordinary spear, bow and arrows and a knife.

Qayaq paddled and paddled.

Somewhere close to the head of Selawik River, Qayaq saw a neat dwelling made of twigs and mud. It was inhabited and he went to it. In this clean home lived a man with his family. Qayaq was invited to stay. The oldest child of the family was a young beautiful girl, a very delicate and dainty person. She became

Spearing Char
Helen Kalvak

Qayaq's wife. As time went on, Qayaq noticed that the father of the family did not bring any animals home when he went out hunting. He brought home little seeds and grubs gathered from the ground. On these the family nibbled. Qayaq nibbled, also. Soon his man-sized body needed more substantial food. So one day he went hunting and brought home many snowshoe rabbits.

He had left his packsack in the shed and the wife, with the rest of the family, went out to inspect it. Qayaq was sitting in the main room when he heard a lot of commotion as if people were struggling with a heavy load. He opened the door to look. There the whole family had pulled one rabbit out from the rest. Pulling it by its hind legs, they struggled with it as if it were as large as a caribou. This made Qayaq impatient. He went out and grabbed the rabbit and threw it into the house, grabbed another and did the same, and another and another. He threw them all in while the father of the family warned his family:

Uh, uh, uh don't let him hurt you!
Uh, uh, uh don't let him hurt you!
Atniqsitna sri, atniqsitna sri!

As one rabbit got thrown near one of the young members of the family, it touched her, and she shrieked in pain. Qayaq went to examine her arm and it was broken. He touched it and straightened it and told her that it would be fine. He skinned one of the rabbits and roasted it over the open fire and passed pieces to each one of the family. On these they nibbled. He ate as much as he could, which was most of a good-sized share. He ate until he was full.

When night time came he fell asleep ahead of the others, tired out from hunting. He seemed to have slept a little while when he was aroused by the words of the father of the family.

"My daughter uh, *paniy uh*, my daughter uh, *paniy ush*, the weather is never the same. This man is a monster. What will happen to him if the time comes when we do not have much? Uh." Woefully, the father was giving his daughter well-meaning advice.

Qayaq went back to sleep. When the morning came he made ready to go. He took the weapons he brought with him: the three-pronged spear, the ordinary spear, bow and arrows, a knife, and the double-bladed hatchet to cut wood, which he had been given by the father of this family. He took his kayak, too.

Qayaq took everything he owned. Noticing this his wife begged him not to go. She was tearful when she said to him, "You take a few steps and look back. You will know what we are."

Qayaq did as he was told. He took a few steps and looked back. There on a stump of a tree was a neat nest made of twigs and mud. On its rim sat a family of hawks. One of them was in grief, her head was hanging down. One of them had a wing that looked like it was injured. Qayaq left them without turning back again.

Qayaq paddled and paddled.

For many days, Qayaq paddled against the strong current of the Selawik River. When he finally reached the mountains that are at the head of the river, he pulled his kayak high up on the bank and resumed his travel north on foot.

Qayaq walked and walked.

Early spring found him climbing a large mountain between the

Transformed Bird
Thomassie Echaluk

Selawik and Kobuk rivers. Climbing up toward what appeared to him like dwellings among the rocks, he saw many many igloos. As he neared them, he heard laughter and the babbling of many voices. He was glad that he was to be with people. While he was still at a distance from the igloos, some people saw him and they ran to meet him. They took his sled from him and pulled it for him the rest of the way.

One man among them invited Qayaq to stay with him. He was a bachelor, and lived alone. These people never seemed to wander far from their homes. His host told Qayaq they were afraid to go too far for fear of animals that might hunt and kill them. Not only animals hunted them, however. His host pointed out to him that some men hunted them, too. At this remark, Qayaq wondered what kind of animals appeared to him as humans this time.

Now and then, more often than seemed natural, a woman would die and be carried away by her mourning family. Qayaq wondered about this.

"They are our women who have been bearing babies," his host told him. "Everytime that a baby is born, it happens. The mother, when she is cut to release the baby, dies."

Qayaq thought this over a long time. He knew he was born but his mother did not die at his birth. He was her twelfth child!

"I better do something about this," he thought. These people he liked very much and they were very good to him.

Not very far from the bachelor's house was a man with six sons and one daughter. The daughter was very beautiful. Qayaq wondered if the father would refuse if he asked for her hand.

He asked his host to take his proposal to the girl's father. The host returned with the message that the father would be very proud if Qayaq would become his son-in-law.

When the wife's pregnancy became apparent, the brothers and

the father were grieved. For many days, they mourned over her. She was the only girl of the family. The girl did not grieve with them. She was very brave and told her relatives that she would live again through her coming child. To the family's grief, Qayaq paid no attention. "I am quite sure I can save her," he thought.

"What sort of a husband is he! Isn't he going to grieve over his wife?" Those words were whispered about the village. Qayaq knew what was being said about him. His wife grew larger with her child. When she looked as if she was getting close to the time of the child's birth, the father gave Qayaq a big knife. When Qayaq hesitated to touch the big knife, the wife said with a smile, "Go ahead, take it, my husband. I am not afraid. I shall live again through my child."

Every day a little at a time, he sharpened the knife. The girl sat by him and had many things to talk about, unconcerned about the knife. Very good-natured and pretty, she chattered on. She seemed always to have something to talk about to her husband. Qayaq learned to love her even more in these days as her ordeal neared. Although she thought each day was bringing her closer to her death, she met each one with the bright clear eyes of a happy girl who cannot wait to hold her first-born in her eager arms. But in her mind, she told herself that she must die. There could be no other way.

One gray morning, she woke her husband. "Wake up, my husband, my time has come!" Qayaq got up and sat beside his wife. Her labor pains came on steadily and she asked him when he was going to get the knife and save the baby.

"I am not going to get the knife," Qayaq replied. "Why should I?

Untitled [Kayak]
Pitseolak Ashoona

I know a better way. I will help you give your baby a natural birth. And you will both live and you will watch your baby grow up."

Now Qayaq woke the rest of the family and told them to gather all the people in the village. When the people came, some of them gaped at him sleepily, speechless in their surprise. "What has happened to you? Do you want everybody to see you use the big knife your father-in-law gave you?" They asked.

"No, no," Qayaq answered. "Just watch."

Then he directed his father-in-law to set up a skin tent for him outdoors.* The father-in-law pulled out the *ee-chuck-sutt*, and Qayaq helped him set it up outdoors. They could hear the brothers shouting at the sleeping people. Climbing up on the roofs of the igloos, the brothers shouted down at them through the skylights. Spreading the news of a baby being born, they shouted, "The mother is going to live too!"

Qayaq's wife walked slowly out of the igloo into the tent. Her wonderful husband had said that she was to have her life, and live on with her brothers, father, and the baby! This made her so very brave that she forgot her pains.

Yes, this was a great day for Qayaq. He was to see his first child. And he was going to be able to save his wife and help save all the other women in the village who would bear children in the future.

Qayaq had them raise the walls of the skin tent. Everyone saw how he helped his wife. Every move had a purpose. Every word had a meaning. He was not nervous, he was not going to rush with it. Witnessed by many unblinking eyes staring and many mouths open, Qayaq's son was born. The mother was alive; she could hardly believe that she was alive. She laughed gratefully at her baby, and seeing the people standing about, laughed and cried too. Everyone was expressing his gratitude for the life of the mother. Now for the first time the mother and the baby were both living.

*This special tent in which a baby is born is traditionally made of six skins sewn together. This tent is called *ee-chuck-sutt*. No matter what animal skin was used, the tent was always made out of six skins. The word "*ee-chuck-sutt*" is used today as the word for the number "six" although its literal meaning is "a covering overhead."

LELA KIANA OMAN

After this, for a while every expectant mother sent for Qayaq when her time came. If he happened to be out with the hunters, a runner was sent after him. Now Qayaq's specialty was helping mothers deliver babies. Every baby opened his eyes for the first time to look into Qayaq's face. He had won the love of everybody. Many gave him gifts that he never failed to show appreciation for.

Among the gifts was an arrow tip with four dull corners. All the arrow tips he had seen were always sharp enough to draw blood when they struck. This he knew was a tip that would strike with a great force, the terrific force that a bow and arrow can give. The name of it was *kutvak*.

Arctic Madonna
Pitaloosie Saila

As the months passed, others learned how to help an expectant mother when the time came for her child to be born. And as the days went by Qayaq was beginning to be very restless. He tried not to be but no matter what he did, he was not satisfied. Then one day he said to his wife, "I must go on now. I would like to stay but I am very restless. This restlessness will not leave me unless I go."

The wilderness in its vastness beckoned him. New, unimaginable excitements awaited him from all corners of the unexplored world. Though what they were going to be, of course, he could not tell.

"I am sorry to see you go. If it was in my power I would make you stay. But as it is, you are not my kind. Sooner or later you must know what we really are. I am not going to grieve over your departure. May you always be lucky, for you have made us very happy." Qayaq's second wife bid him farewell without tears.

Then Qayaq said, "As for our child, I may wish to have him with me in the future." Qayaq loved his son very much. It was said that later when he had a human wife his soul came for this son and he was born to his human wife as a baby. This was supposed to be the beginning of "choosing babies from all kinds of animals."

"Not very far from here when you look back, we will appear to you as we really are," she told him.

Everybody in the settlement was notified of Qayaq's going. Everybody gathered to see him off. A few young men were chosen to help him pull his sled over the rocks down the slope of the mountain.

With many good wishes ringing in his ears, he left them. When they reached the ground that was not rugged, his escorts bade him farewell and turned back and slowly climbed the mountain. Qayaq sat on his sled and watched them awhile.

When he reached the bottom of the mountain, he looked back. Half way up the mountain were many large rocks. Among them he saw many mountain sheep. The slope of the mountain was white with them. Many years ago the mountain sheep were known to appear as human beings.

QAYAQ VISITS THE UMIALIK'S VILLAGE. THE INFLUENCE OF ANCESTORS IS PARTICULARLY STRESSED

Qayaq walked and walked.

From mountain to mountain he travelled, pulling his sled behind him. Up on top of these mountains he noticed old frames of old boats, large and small. They appeared to have been beached. At one time the water must have been very high, and the big boats left there to decay. They were not found on some mountains, but on other mountains they lay weather-beaten and bleached like skeletons of animals. They had been there for so long that the sod and grass grew on them.

Finally as he started descending a mountain, he saw the Kobuk River. On a high bluff overlooking this wide river was a village with the mounds of many sod-covered houses. People were walking on its many paths. He thought that surely, the people walking on the paths were human. When he was still about a mile away from the village he stopped on a little ridge to watch them.

On a flat place between the village and the mountain some young people were playing ball. They would kick a skin ball and run after it, everyone chasing it. The first one reaching the ball would kick it again so that the chase kept going and going. The players were so absorbed in the game that they did not notice a stranger watching them.

A little lower down the mountainside than the ridge where Qayaq was standing was another ridge with the mound of an Eskimo house on it. Two people were sitting in front of its tunnel entrance. Spruce trees grew close to the house as well as everywhere on the mountainside. It was now fall. At this time of year, their deep green was broken here and there by the golden leaves of aspen on the mountain and willows by the river.

Qayaq, with his sled trailing behind him, went over rocks and sod and descended the mountain, heading for the solitary hut. Over the bare ground he pulled his sled easily. He was so strong he could have pulled it over anything. Down to the sitting figures he made his way. When he was within hearing distance, he heard a weeping sound. "I wonder what those two are weeping over," Qayaq said to himself.

"Eee-ee-eee-ee." The weeping sound was coming to his ears louder and louder. *"Eckneek uh."* Some of the words he could understand now. *"Eek-neeng* (my son), you are not breathing today. He had no cause to kill you. We cannot avenge your death. Only thing we can do now is waste away by grieving over you."

A few yards away from the weeping pair, Qayaq stopped. Though he was so near them, they did not notice him. Finally, Qayaq said, "What are you crying about?" The two stopped crying suddenly and acted as if they were surprised to hear a voice. "I want to know what you are crying about," Qayaq continued.

"We cannot see you, we are both blind from weeping over our son," the husband answered. "My wife can see the outlines of objects but I am stone blind. Who are you, and where did you come from?"

"I am sorry you heard us weeping, but our weeping we cannot do anything about," the wife added. "Our son was killed in a combat with the village *Umialik*.* That Umialik, he asked for our son to be his son-in-law, then he had him killed. He has many different and cruel ways to kill a son-in-law."

"I would like to meet this Umialik," Qayaq thought to himself. "Would you let me stay with you for awhile?" Qayaq asked aloud to the man and wife. Qayaq wanted to stay very much. He might be able to do something about the village Umialik. He faced the little mounds which appeared to be the dwellings which covered the elevated ground.

On the river side of the village was a cliff which fell straight down to the depth of the river. It appeared to him as if it had many victims and many secrets that it did not mean to reveal. But the secrets of this cliff were not hidden from Qayaq, who gazed upon it with eyes that could look into a man's soul.

The elderly couple were glad to have him. When evening came, he prepared food for his host and hostess from his sled. His sled was always heaped with food, food that he had gathered on his journey. "This is the first time that somebody has showed us kindness since our son was killed," the husband commented as he swallowed hard in the act of fighting back the tears. As for Qayaq, he enjoyed his company, for he had not seen anybody for some time.

When morning came, he heard something outside. Somebody

* Umialik means Chief, a spokesman of many village gatherings, and a rich man. To be rich a man would go to Qikigtagruk (Kotzebue) and come home with pokes (containers made of sealskin) of seal oil, rawhide ropes and *ugruk* (bearded seal) skins for *mukluk* (boot) bottoms.

was coming on the run. When the runner reached the little hut, he stopped. The old man heard him and cried, "Who are you? What do you want?"

"I am from the village. Umialik would like to see your visitor," the intruder answered.

"Now that he knows that you are here, he will not give you any rest unless you satisfy him with your appearance," the old man told Qayaq. "Do whatever you think is best. You do not have to obey if you do not want to."

"I will go. I am anxious to meet him," said Qayaq. He was not afraid.

He made ready and, taking his sled, he followed the messenger to the village. Among many huts was a large one, a chief's house. Larger and higher its rounded roof stood than the rounded roofs of the other homes of the village. They entered a large house with a dome-like ceiling and round-shaped floor. It was lighted by four seal oil lamps. On one side were boys sitting on the floor and on the other side to Qayaq's left were girls. The girls were dressed in parkas made of caribou, which were caught in the summer and tanned so that they were very soft. On the borders of the coat and sleeves were delicate designs of different shades and kinds of cut fur. A little apart from the other girls sat a beautiful gentle looking girl. She raised her head from her sewing long enough to give Qayaq a brief smile and went on with her work. Two long braids, black and shiny, hung down her sides, and half their lengths rested on the black shiny caribou skin that was her mat.

"She shall be my wife. I am going to live just to have this beautiful girl for my mate," Qayaq vowed to himself.

A large man was lying flat on his stomach with a big fur pillow under his chest, elbows on the floor, his chin cupped in his palms. In front of him was the choicest food that could be obtained.

Berries, dried meats and *muktuk* (whale skin) were set before him. Dressed in an elaborately-made parka of caribou skins, he nibbled on the food. With his feet against the wall, he lay facing the door.

"He is even lazy in the way he eats," Qayaq thought as he watched him. The large man made no indication of having seen Qayaq enter. It was as if he thought the only important thing to do in the world was to keep on eating. His high forehead, bushy eyebrows and generally strong appearance impressed Qayaq. He knew that he was meeting with a man of wisdom and was baffled by the man's not giving him any sign of greeting.

"Why did he send for me?" Qayaq wondered. "Isn't he going to say something to me?" Qayaq felt insulted and disappointed by the indifference of the Umialik. As he lived on with the boys for many days, he had to try to keep down the angry feeling in his heart.

Umialik appeared to be lazy at first, but he was about one of the busiest men Qayaq had ever met. As the days went by, Umialik continued to ignore Qayaq. As the days flew by for Qayaq, his respect for Umialik grew.

When winter came they hunted together along with the boys of the house. Duplicates of Qayaq's weapons were made and adopted by Umialik. For Umialik's only weapons had been spear, knife and a stone hammer. Qayaq brought them three new ones: the bow and arrows he had carried with him from Sauniqtuq, the copper fish-spear he took from the otter-fisherman, and a little double-bladed stone hatchet to cut wood, which he had been given by the hawk family. Qayaq was proud of what he had contributed to these people. Qayaq, however, was not as yet recognized by Umialik as he wanted to be. He kept thinking, "Maybe tomorrow he will address me directly."

They hunted caribou, sheep, wolves and wolverine. Wolf skins and wolverine skins were for trimming parkas, and caribou and sheep were for food and clothing. Qayaq's catch was always larger and fatter than the rest of the boys' catch. He always pulled a heavier load than any of the rest. On one of their hunting trips, Umialik at last called Qayaq to one side and told him to come home with him. When the other young men saw Umialik talking directly to Qayaq, they went on ahead into the mountains to continue hunting. With not a single word, they left Umialik and Qayaq. They knew Umialik had chosen Qayaq to be his son-in-law and that Umialik would not hunt any more that day. On their way home Umialik told Qayaq that he had proved worthy of being his son-in-law.

After the hunt that day, the boys did not return to the Umialik's house, as had been their custom. Qayaq noticed that they had all gone back to their families. They had all been on trial as prospective in-laws to the man. Now that Qayaq was chosen, they understood their dismissal.

Qayaq and the beautiful seamstress became husband and wife.

The girls waited on Umialik and Qayaq. Qayaq was never given a chance to even get a drink of water for himself. This made him irritable. Umialik, noticing this, kept him out hunting many days at a time. On these hunting trips, Qayaq was always the better hunter. About this Umialik was not happy.

"I will hunt alone today," he decided one early morning. To this Qayaq nodded and dismissed the idea from his mind. Umialik's daughter knew why her father had gone off alone, and she made up her mind that she was going to do something about it. She took her husband outside and pointed to a big cliff not far from the set-tlement, but far enough so you could not see a man if he was there.

"That is where my father gets his help. At the bottom of the cliff live the souls of the people who drowned during the Big Flood; these souls are called *Iqsingat* (First To Know Fear).

"I do not like to speak against my father," she said. "But I have decided to do so because, with my father's departure alone today, I know your life is in danger. He chooses husbands for me, and just when I have learned to love a man, somehow or other he is killed. I am allowed to show no sign of mourning but my heart is heavy from losing my husbands."

"The souls that live under that cliff are very fond of wolverine fur. Umialik took a strip of wolverine with him. That is why I know he was going to visit them. Without their help he has no power. I am giving you a chance to escape this treacherous father of mine. He is my father and I shall handle him myself, if you wish to escape. I will give myself up to be destroyed by his anger. At least I shall know that my loved one lives on."

Qayaq told his wife that he was not afraid. "Only tell me about the Big Flood and why the cliff is inhabited by the souls. I am sure I will be able to conquer Umialik. I would be ashamed to be a murderer of my wife's father but, if it is the only way out, you must forgive me. Fighting for my life, however, I shall fight for his, too. I have learned to respect him. I shall try to meet any challenge he makes to me, but I shall try to do so without harming him."

Qayaq was very curious about the Big Flood. Back inside the house again, the wife began the story.

THE STORY OF THE BIG FLOOD
AS IT WAS TOLD
BY QAYAQ'S WIFE

Many, many years ago there were many people on this earth. All these little hills were covered with many dwellings. Along these rivers, big settlements were set up. The rain and the sunshine came in every frequency. But the spirit that controlled the rains was not pleased. Somebody had done something to make him angry. He was so very angry that he brought rains.

It seemed that it was going to rain forever. The people were beginning to be taking it for granted. But to their horror, the rivers and lakes began to swell beyond their banks. They overflowed and flooded the plains. People living on the plains began to seek refuge on the hills. With their big boats they moved from hill to hill and when the hills were submerged they moved from mountain to mountain.

Among them some were caught by whirlpools and, of course, they could not fight the whirlpools and their boats capsized and many, many people lost their lives.

One good-sized settlement had beliefs of having powers taken from certain animals and birds. Some believed in bears and wolves and sea animals. Among them lived a person who claimed to have power taken from a bird named Tulugaq, a black bird, a raven, so very black that it was slightly blue. Raven tried so hard to steal fire from the humans that he burnt himself black and he tried so hard to rub out the smoke from himself that he went a little crazy. A little bit absent-minded, this Raven Man was slow to make decisions, so that others were always beating him in doing something. In hunting he was so slow that he always had to take the leftovers at meals. This man had two wives and many children. They were the poorest family in the settlement. He talked about it all so much that his neighbours nicknamed him Tulugaq.

This group lived in their boats and moved from mountain to mountain. Soon the mountaintops were the only land visible. Finally there was only one mountaintop left. The people realized that the one they occupied was the only one. All the others were submerged except the one they were on.

The Flood
Ruth Annaqtuusi Tulurialik

THE EPIC OF QAYAQ 25

One early morning as they watched to see if they would be given a sign, they saw something swimming in the water. In a split second it came up and it went down again. Every day, as their land became smaller and smaller, the object would come and show itself for just a flash.

The wise men gathered together and made up their minds the best thing to do was to try to catch the object that showed itself once a day.

Each man called for help from his helping spirit. All kinds of birds and animals were called upon by their believers, but no one caught the swimming object.

The Raven Man did not pay any attention to this because as usual he was loafing and not paying attention to what was really happening.

The people became a little more discouraged. Finally some one said, "What about Tulugaq, he has not done anything so far!" But he did not pay any attention to their pleading.

"We have lost all we had. We have lost our homes and the many things that we had acquired by working hard. What is there left to live for!" Thus Tulugaq answered their plea, and kept on loafing.

They were on this little tiny island, formerly a mountaintop. The water was still rising, closing in on them. Women and children faced certain death if something was not done. Everyone who claimed to have supernatural power — everyone but Tulugaq, the Raven Man — made a try at catching the unknown object that was showing itself in the water each day. But no one was quick enough to spear it.

"If you men cannot do it, how can I! I was always the slowest in catching anything. I would only make a fool of myself if I tried." So the lazy Tulugaq would answer any of them who tried to get him to take a chance along with the rest of them at catching the unknown object.

L E L A   K I A N A   O M A N

His two wives begged him, when no one else could make him move. "You do not care what happens to us. Can't you see all your children will drown? Try anyway, it will be easier to die knowing that you have tried."

"I will try just once and I shall not try again," Tulugaq declared.

Many now were living in their boats, for there was no room on the land for them. When Tulugaq made ready to try, he sat down in his kayak. Now there was room enough for his two wives on the little piece of dry land. They knelt down and began to sing. Closing their eyes, hands on their knees, legs folded under them, they sang:

Tulugaq, black bird with blackest of wings,
You have always been the weakest, the slowest and the
most humble.
Now is the time.
You can be strong, fast and proud.
Here is the time you can do something.
li ya ya yay, ii ya ya yay

Tulugaq paddled away in his kayak. The surface of the water was glassy and golden as the sun shone down with not a slightest bit of shade after many days of rain. Tulugaq could hear his two wives. He knew that they were putting all they had behind him. He must do his very best. He did not have to wait very long. He saw it in the water, a round object coming up fast. He measured its speed in his mind and, heading it off, he gave a few big strokes with his paddle and closing his eyes he sent his spear with all the power he had.

He heard shouting from behind. "You caught it! You have saved us from drowning." Tulugaq opened his eyes … and there in front

Tulugak
Agnes Nanogak

of him was a huge tussock with a spear struck through it. The water was falling away fast from it! The tussock was shooting skyward. Water was rolling away from the little piece of land that their boats were on and Tulugaq's two wives were still singing:

Tulugaq has speared a *haayugaq*
(top of a submerged mountain).
We are proud that we are his wives.
Today we are the two proudest women.
li ya ya yay ii ya ya yay

People paddled hard. They had a hard time keeping up with the water's edge, as the tops of the mountains came into view again. They could not even sleep, following the water down to the valley bottom as it quickly receded. If they stopped to rest, their boats would have been left high and dry on the side of the mountain.

"I am telling you this story, though my father would not wish me to do so," said Qayaq's wife. How beautiful she looked sitting there on her black caribou mat, her two long braids hanging down on her sides, half their length lying out on the black shiny caribou skin that was her mat.

"Go on, you are not telling it without cause. Our future may depend on it," Qayaq said gently. Qayaq's third wife, he was sure, was human and she was dear to him.

His wife went on with the story. She said, "The boats of the people who perished in the Big Flood can be found on tops of the mountains.

"The people starting from Tulugaq became a clan, enlarged in number and scattered everywhere. These people became shiftless. From day to day they feared that another flood might come again and take away from them everything they had worked hard to gain.

"Many, many years later the flood was gradually forgotten but still the people lived for just today. Now they were not expecting anything to extinguish them from the face of the earth but still they lived from day to day doing nothing but hunting and, of course, finding new ways to improve their supernatural powers. For it was only their supernatural powers that had saved them from the flood.

"Then, many generations later there lived a man who claimed to have power given to him by his relatives who had died. 'Through me my ancestors, my protectors, drink and eat again,' he would say.

"One day this extraordinary man wandered in his kayak farther away from home than usual. On his way home he had to pass a high cliff that towered over a river. Its gray stone face stood on the edge of the Kobuk River. Before he reached this cliff, night overtook him. But as he neared the big cliff, he saw a bright light in the very heart of it. At first he was frightened. Then two men in kayaks met him and led him inside the cliff. There he saw many thin women, men and children. They appeared to have lived there for many years.

"'Do not be afraid!' A man who seemed to be the oldest was their spokesman. 'We do not mean to frighten you. We have tried to get the notice of living people for many years, but we have never seen anyone besides you that believed in the Living Dead. We have watched you taking strength from your ancestors. They are the souls of the dead like we are, but they cannot be with us. They are far removed from us. We believe we are the oldest souls that can ever get in contact with the living people. We are the souls who perished in the Big Flood. We have no children to carry on our souls. We are the *Iqsingat*. When you have plenty to eat, we have hardly any. When you are at the point of starvation, there is plenty of food that is bestowed upon us. We are having a hard time now. See how thin we are? That is why we lured you here. In your hunting trips when you happen to catch plenty, you will know that we catch nothing. At such times you will leave a little at this cliff. In our sight it will multiply into plenty.'

"They did not want him to touch anything in their dwelling. They did not allow him to eat either, for if he did, he would become one of them.

"He noticed that he was not given a chance to speak. He was led out of the cliff, and out on the river he turned around and saw again the big steep rock walls of the high cliff. An unusual thing had happened to him he knew.

"After that, this man on his way home from a hunting trip would stop at the steep cliff and leave little pieces of meat hanging on a little piece of protruding rock. The next day the meat would be gone.

"This man who had claimed to have power given him by his ancestors knew now something extraordinary was happening in that steep cliff.

"From time to time he was led into the interior of the cliff. The souls of the people who perished in the Big Flood were given the privilege of coming into contact with the living through this strong shaman.

"These souls still are there and my father has gone to see them today, hoping they will accept a strip of wolverine fur. If they accept the strip, it will multiply into many wolverine skins. Many times they are not satisfied, no matter what the gift. And sometimes they do not appear to the living for many years," Qayaq's wife said.

That night Qayaq lay wide-awake, thinking of all his wife had told him. Why didn't his parents tell him about the Flood? He knew that the practice of shamanism was started by the people who came from the Western Mountain. Would Tulugaq, the Raven Man who caught the tussock, have claimed to have received his power from the raven, unless he was from the Western Mountain like Qayaq's own father?* What his wife told him must be true, too, because he had run across the evidence, the skeletons of the big and small boats high and dry up on tops of the mountains.

Maybe his parents were so absorbed in their grief over losing their sons that they had not thought to tell him. But he knew that his father was the descendant of the Western Mountain and his mother the descendant of the Eastern Mountain. He knew the Big Flood had occurred after the people from these two mountains met and made their living together.

Qayaq pictured in his mind the invited guest of the *Iqsingat*, (First to know Fear), a man in his kayak in the midst of their dwelling, the interior of a cliff. The light that seemed to come from nowhere and the people the man had never seen before encircling him all around, their eyes straining at him. He was the center of their attention. Yes, Qayaq knew he had run across something that was extraordinary.

The woman who told him of all this was sleeping beside him and in the same room his father-in-law slept noisily. He could hear him now puffing and snorting in his sleep. How easy it would be for him to reach for his bow and arrow and shoot in the direction of the loud breathing sounds.

But Qayaq would not do that. For one thing he was anxious to learn of the rituals that his father-in-law must follow to try to get rid of a son-in-law. Born to be in love with adventure, Qayaq was

*Tulugaq was a shaman and it was believed that he had received his power from the raven, taken by him as his helper through the practice of shamanism.

again excited as he stared into the darkness of the room with eyes that were steady and that could penetrate darkness and could see into a man's soul.

All that winter Qayaq and his father-in-law hunted. Sometimes together and sometimes they took turns.

Toward the spring Umialik began to make his helpers prepare a feast. Everybody in the little settlement was to attend this. There would be games and feats of skill.

The most important and the most fun that people looked forward to was a jumping-board contest. Umialik liked this game very much and he was known to compete with every man. He felt at home on the board. It was as if he was born just for the athletic feat of jumping on it.

Every game lasted a day. Qayaq participated in any games that he was called to be a contestant in. Most of the time his name was not called. The people appeared to look upon him as an outsider, one that was not one of them. Whether he won a game or not did not count. They looked upon him as not one of them. They did not even care to know where he came from. To this Qayaq was indifferent as he looked upon them as people who had been forced to adopt him.

The jumping-board game was the last one to be played, and the one that every one most looked forward to. Everyone came out to watch it. Umialik was going to jump with every man who wanted to jump on the teeter-totter board.

A large rock was laid on the cliff a few feet away from the edge. The cliff stood high above a deep chasm. It was not likely that anybody would be allowed to fall off the jumping-board, over the cliff and into the chasm. Every man trusted the Umialik not to let that happen.

This jumping-board is like a big see-saw or teeter-totter board. At each end of the board a man stands ready to be thrown into the air. When he comes down he lands on his end of the board and throws the other man high into the air. The man that loses his balance and falls off the board is the loser.

Umialik played this jumping-board game all day. He never lost his balance and no matter how expert the other fellow was on the other end of the board, Umialik managed to make him lose his balance.

Everyone had taken a try and there was no one left to jump against him.

Umialik called on his son-in-law, "Come on, see if you can throw me off my balance."

Qayaq came without hesitating. He respected his father-in-law very much. He would not refuse him. Qayaq climbed on the board and stood on the end ready to be thrown into the air. The board see-sawed steady for a few times. Qayaq felt the board under him and steadying himself, he jumped up into the air at the same time that he was thrown upwards by his opponent. Coming down, he landed on the board and sent his father-in-law high into the air. In mid-air he saw his father-in-law struggling a little. Nearing the board Umialik righted himself and landed on his end of the board with everything he had. Qayaq felt himself being thrown high. He heard the onlookers shouting and screaming. That this match was unusual Qayaq knew by the increased shouting and screaming of the spectators. He landed with his two feet on the board and saw Umialik being thrown into the air again. Way up in the air Umialik turned a somersault. The crowd roared with delight. They were laughing and shouting.

But as the jumping contest continued, it began to look as if Umialik was losing his championship. He was aware that he was not showing as much strength as Qayaq. He could hear some people shouting in favor of Qayaq. If he lost this contest, the people would look for a stronger man to be their Umialik. Qayaq saw that his

Standing Bird
with Outstreched Wings
Annie Arragutainaq

father-in-law was coming down on the jumping-board with his eyes black with rage and his mouth set in a straight, determined line. Their eyes met for a split second. Qayaq saw what was in Umialik's mind. Umialik righted himself and as he landed kicked the board to his left with all the power that was in him. Qayaq felt himself being thrown into the air off to the left. He realized he was missing the board, missing the ground, falling over the cliff. Nobody was shouting. The crowd was silenced by what they saw.

Qayaq saw the cliff side. He was falling fast and the bottom was rushing up to meet him. Then before he landed, he quickly turned into a little hawk. He sat at the bottom for a little while, getting his breath back. Then he flew around the cliff and made his way to Umialik's house which was now also his home. At the door he shook off the bird appearance and turned back into himself. He made his way into the house and sat down by his wife who was sewing.

In a little while they heard a running sound, the ground shook as the men ran. They heard a man coming in, all breathless from running. He opened the door and looked in. A young man gave a laugh and turned around and ran out.

"He is alive, he is sitting with his wife!" They heard him shouting. Many had run, for Umialik had told them the one who reached the house first would have his daughter for his wife.

Umialik's daughter looked at Qayaq with a question in her eyes, but Qayaq met her eyes with a smile and did not say a word. She understood his silent answer. He made it plain he was not going to talk about it. She knew Qayaq had escaped her treacherous father's effort to kill him. She calmly went on with her sewing, pretending

not to notice the excitement that was in every vil-
lager that day.

There was to be a big feast and her girl helpers
were preparing for it. They were busy with making
akutuq and cutting up dried meats. All kinds of
berries had to be taken in from the cache. All the
many kinds of food that could be obtained in that
country were to be eaten that day.

Everyone was to come and eat in Umialik's house.
This was the greatest event of the year.

Umialik came home from the jumping-board game.
He came in and made his way to his own corner
of the house. He sat down on his sleeping couch and
turned his face to the wall. He was breathing in racking
deep breaths. His daughter knew he was displeased.
He had tried to maneuver a son-in-law to his death
and for the first time he had failed.

Qayaq sat beside his wife without any anxiety
for his father-in-law's state of mind. Hate was not
in Qayaq's heart. He was sent out by his parents prepared to
overcome anything that was evil.

Gradually Umialik recovered from his disappointment. And
soon Qayaq and his father-in-law hunted together again.

On one of their hunting trips Umialik took Qayaq to the top of
a mountain. Facing north he pointed out to the tops of the mountains
that were hardly visible.

"Beyond these mountains is a bird with one foot. Its meat is
very tasty." The old man licked his lips pretending to anticipate
the tastiness of the bird. "Ah, how I would like to eat some now!"
With a faraway look in his eyes he licked his lips again. His old
shriveled up lips were once more straight in a determined line. How

One-footed Bird
Edith Akoluk

very crafty, cunning, and old he looked standing there, gazing at those faraway mountains and speaking of the tasty bird who lived beyond those peaks far to the north.

Qayaq could not help feeling sorry for his father-in-law, as Umialik pointed out to him the location of the one-footed bird. With his gnarled hand, he looked very pitifully old.

"I can go and get the bird for you if you want it," Qayaq said. He meant what he promised. He respected his father-in-law just as much as he loved his wife.

He respected his father-in-law for many things. He had become the Umialik of his clan. He had made his way up to the highest place that could be given by his people. His word was the law and his happiness, the happiness of his followers. People that could, went out of their way to please him. A pleased smile on his face was the only reward they ever expected to receive. Above all, Qayaq respected Umialik because he had the power to come in contact with the souls of the people who perished in the Big Flood.

"If you run, that is two days travelling. I am sure you will not have any trouble killing the one-footed bird," said Umialik convincingly.

The next morning when Qayaq went out of the house it was still dark. Toward the east he noticed the dawn giving its first yawn, the beginning of a new day.

Qayaq walked and walked.

The early morning was frosty, the sky very blue and he could hear the crunchy sound his feet made in the dry snow.

Qayaq took a taste of the *akutuq* his mother made, and he felt on his right side the caressing of the soft east wind. "My wind is a very kind wind." He was hearing his mother's words again. As he faced the north, he began to run, seeing again in his mind his parting with his parents. He wondered how they were getting along. How very easy it would be for him to turn around and be on the run straight for home. He longed to see his parents and he vowed to himself that some day... some day he was going home to see them. But now he had something else to do.

All that day he ran, stopping just long enough to rest and to eat. When the night came he was still on the run over many hills, stretches of tundra and high mountains.

The afternoon of the second day, he saw from the top of a mountain a big flat space ahead of him. All around this flat space were mountains, very tall mountains. In the middle of the flat space he saw it: the one-footed bird. As his father-in-law had told him, it was so very black and large that he had no trouble seeing it. The bird had seen him first and was speeding toward him.

This bird, even though one-footed, could make its way very quickly. The bird and Qayaq sped toward each other. The bird hopped long distances on its one foot helped by its two flapping wings which dug into the snow on each side of it. The wings were too short to lift the heavy bird off the snow but long enough to dig into the crust and to throw chunks of snow and ice all around it.

When the great bird came within the range of Qayaq's arrows, he sent one with a terrific force behind it. To his horror he saw his arrow land on its mark and skim away without any effect on the snorting and fuming and speeding bird. As the bird ran nearer he showered it with arrows. The arrows struck terrific blows on many places on the big bird but the bird seemed not to be affected. Qayaq saw its eyes, big fiery eyes, very close now. Too terribly close. The only weapon Qayaq had besides his bow and arrows was his stone knife. There was no turning back. This one-footed bird was speeding toward him and he stood there waiting for it, a stone knife in his hand. For the first time, he felt his great heart pounding in fright. But there was no turning back. He knew that he was going to have to fight hard for his life. One of them was soon to die.

The big black bird opened its beak in the act of swallowing Qayaq. Qayaq with all his strength struck the bird on its head. And he heard the sound of rock striking rock. Then Qayaq lost consciousness.

When Qayaq opened his eyes, he was riding the bird. His legs and arms were entwined around the neck of the big bird. The wind in his ears was buzzing. His body ached and he heard above him the song, the song that his father had given him. What a fool he had been not to think of that in the first place! The bird kept hopping and flapping in its awkward gait, jarring Qayaq with sickening violence. The bird tried to make its gait more uneven and rough in an effort to shake Qayaq off its back.

Qayaq knew that his father's song of power was helping him. Even though he had slipped so that he was now hanging down in front of the bird, no part of him was dragging on the ground, or getting hurt by sharp ice and rocks. With his knife he kept striking the bird, with each blow hearing the sound of rock striking rock. This flint knife made a cracking sound when it hit the bird's stone feathers.

What could he do? From the underside of the neck of the bird he worked his way to a flapping wing. Perhaps this would be more vulnerable. Not a spot on this bird was not covered with feathers of rock or scales of rock.

The bird still sped on. When it reached the other side of the flat, it turned around and raced back to the other end again, trying to shake Qayaq off. Riding the violent winged steed, Qayaq hacked away at the black rock armor that was the bird's covering.

When night came, they were still fighting, the bird stamping around now in a circle. Half-crazy with anger, it still kept trying to shake Qayaq off. Qayaq, almost fainting with fatigue, still hacked away at the stone scales. He crawled over its wings, its back. Every inch of the bird, he covered — finally and at last, he was letting himself down its strong leg toward the single foot. He thought to himself that he was about to give up. When he reached the scaly joint of the foot, he struck. With a great shriek, the big bird toppled over. Qayaq saw blood spurting from the wound. It spurted over him, covering him with blood.

The one-footed bird was breathing its last breath as the last ounce of its blood ebbed away from its big body. Qayaq walked a little way, fell down on the snow and sank into a deep sleep.

His wife's father, Umialik, had sent him to kill the bird, pretending to know that its meat was tasty. No one had ever survived when this bird with one foot and scales of stone laid its fiery eyes upon him. Qayaq wondered how many animals and men had lost their lives, on this great wilderness flatland, inhabited for so many years only by this bird. How many young men had Umialik sent here to be killed? How did Umialik know that the bird was here? It was because he thought that Qayaq would certainly be killed that Umialik had sent him here.

When Qayaq opened his eyes, the sun was high and warm. His body ached with every move he made. He was encrusted with the clots of blood from the bird. There, just a little way from him lay the bird. Like a big gray hill it lay.

He examined the bird and tried to cut a piece to take home with him, but his knife could not cut even the tiniest piece of it. He himself all crusted with the bird's blood was evidence enough to convince his father-in-law that he had killed his tasty one-footed bird.

Qayaq made his way home not caring when he reached home.

Dance
Helen Kalvak

He took his time. He was not on the run this time.

It took him four days to get back to his home. The sun was sinking down to the western horizon when he came in sight of the little settlement. Slowly he made his way down to the bluff. No one was out of doors and Qayaq wondered what had happened. As he neared the big domelike house of Umialik, he heard shouting. He climbed up the house to the sky-light, and looked in through the window made of a seal's *inaluk* (dried intestines). There in Umialik's house, the people were dancing. He could hear Umialik singing a victory song:

If Qayaq were alive, he would be home by now.
We know he is dead.
Anything that the one-footed bird sees cannot escape.
His appetite is too great!
Eee-yah ngah Eee-yah-ngah.
Ooi! Ooi! Ooi!
Ooi! Ooi!

Swelled with pride, Umialik sang, stamping his heel on the smooth hard stone that was the floor. How very happy he looked, standing there singing for his young people, who were absorbed in their strenuous dancing. Older people and children were sitting all around the wall of the house, big enough to serve as a community hall. "Tomorrow is a feast. Everyone shall eat, so Qayaq's soul will not be hungry. The day after, we will dress somebody; so Qayaq's soul can have clothes to wear."

Umialik kept on singing little victory songs and with a little stamping of his foot on the floor, he would finish off each one with "Ooi! Ooi!"

Qayaq saw his wife sitting at her usual place sewing, pretending not to notice the merriment, her head bent over her work; he could not see her face.

Qayaq straightened up. Standing on the top of the house, he saw clouds above him painted pink by the setting sun. A fresh frost was settling over the hard crusty snow. Hills and mountains covered with evergreen trees, some of them here and there slightly gray with the frost, lay peacefully around the little settlement which had such a cruel and treacherous man for its Umialik.

Qayaq stood a long time, living over his fight with the one-footed bird. He had respected his father-in-law very much and loved his wife. So eager was he to please his father-in-law, he had almost lost his life.

If his wife had been dancing along with the young people, he would have gone in there and killed Umialik with his bare hands. In his heart he knew that his wife was grieving for him silently. He was not going to hurt his wife's feelings by killing her father. He bent over the window again and called, in a loud voice, for his wife.

"Bring me some clean clothes to change into."

He saw all the dancers stop and with surprise they all shouted, "His soul! His soul! In death he has come back to haunt us!"

"This is Qayaq in person. I would come in and show you but I am a terrible sight now."

Qayaq's wife came out with the new parka, the new pants and mukluks which she always had ready for him. Helping him take off his bloody clothes, his wife talked to him, "Dear husband, I had a feeling that you were coming back to me. I am so happy that you have escaped one more of my father's death traps. But this will not be the last; he will always try to kill you as long as you are with us. Why don't you go back to the place where you came from?"

Qayaq did not answer. He slipped out of his bloody clothes. His old parka was barely hanging together by a strip of fur here and there. He looked handsome as he put on the new clothes his wife had ready for him.

By this time, the dancers and the audience were filing out of Umialik's big domelike house. They hurried away to their own dwellings, pretending not to notice what had come to pass.

Qayaq and his wife walked into the Umialik's house. How proud the woman was of her husband! She could hear the whispers of the girl-helpers. "Qayaq killed the one-footed bird! If he hadn't, he would not be here." The house was filled with their murmurs.

Qayaq's wife gave the girl-helpers a swift glance. All became quiet; their mistress had given them a silent order. They knew and loved their beautiful mistress. These girls waited on her from morning till night. She loved each one. They understood this and returned her love, showing it in obedience and in their shining eyes. Never, never in words.

These hard-working girls were not servants in any ordinary sense. They were made to feel that they were of the same rank as their mistress. They were her companions and helpers. She worked as hard as they did and felt at ease in chattering with them and they with her, whenever men were not present. When the men folks were home, the women did not speak and express their thoughts nor laugh as they pleased. All the laughing and talking was done by the men folks in the evenings.

The men were out hunting all day. The house belonged to the men in the evening. The women did their work during the evening as if they were deaf and dumb. Moving about with straight and expressionless faces, they only spoke when they were spoken to. To be loud or outspoken was in bad taste. If a woman expressed her thoughts and let everyone see how good-natured she was, she was acting in an undignified way. Every woman understood that she must be reserved and quiet in the presence of men. If she acted otherwise, she was lectured to by an older woman. From the time a girl was old enough to understand, her mother saw to it that she was taught the manners of a lady.

In the excitement of Qayaq's unexpected return these girls forgot their manners in the presence of the Umialik. Umialik felt insulted. Was not Qayaq's return bad enough to take? He took the murmuring of the girls at Qayaq's return as an insult and was greatly displeased. He felt almost ill with anger. Umialik laid himself on his sleeping couch, his face turned to the wall, his muscular shoulders heaving with tortured, racking breaths.

This man who was supposed to have power from all the great shamans that were his ancestors and, in addition, was able to be in contact with the *Iqsingat*, was deeply insulted. He had been very proud of his position as Umialik and had shown his pride and his authority without fear. No one had any right to ridicule him for his behavior. Without ever questioning him, the villagers had seen his ill treatment of his former sons-in-law and that he had just put his present son-in-law to a life-endangering test. He had given Qayaq four days to come back from this test. When Qayaq did not come, he thought the test had been fatal for his son-in-law and therefore, he had thought it was now fitting to give a dance and a feast for his soul.

When given orders by him, his followers obeyed him without hesitation. Umialik knows best, he can never make a mistake. He who is led by an unseen hand and power from the powerful souls of his ancestors, he never makes just his own decisions, and when given an idea to act upon, he must follow the orders of the supernatural. Such words as these were said among the many people in their dwellings. For all of them loved and worshipped him. He, in return, helped and was kind to them in his own selfish way. Much unnecessary suffering caused by Umialik was forgiven readily enough by the people saying, "He knows best. I must be to blame for this suffering."

If Umialik noticed any grudges against him among the villagers he saw to it that he was avenged. Umialik had enjoyed being respected by some and loved by some and obeyed by all. Now Qayaq who refused to be easily killed was an obstacle to his continuing pride in his ability to handle every situation according to his own will. Here was Qayaq, welcomed home by all — even by Umalik's beloved daughter! How very incredible that his own usually obedient daughter was showing happiness over the return of Qayaq! The sight was no comfort to his old injured heart.

Just a little while ago, he had been so very happy singing for his youthful dancers, stamping on the smooth hard floor with his heel, crying "Ooi." It seemed to him that the echo of the victory song was still lingering in the domelike shape of the house. "Ooi, Ooi, Ooi." Umialik had been in the glory of his supremacy then. Now he felt like he could no longer be proud in the presence of his son-in-law.

Qayaq was sitting beside his wife eating the choice food prepared for him. Not far from him his father-in-law lay, his face turned to the wall, his shoulders heaving with tortured, racking breaths. Qayaq looked at the suffering old man and forgave him. He saw him with eyes that looked into his soul. He knew how badly he had injured Umialik's swollen pride. He was very grateful for his wife who was now sitting by his side in silence.

The girls were pattering about silently doing their evening chores. However simple the chores may be, they must be done expertly and with care. Not an irritated sign was breathed. Everyone understood the tension in the house — the young couple eating silently and the old Umialik with his face to the wall grieving alone. But why was he grieving? For the death of the one-footed bird? No one would ask Umialik for they knew he would never be able to explain his hurt. All these people would always obey him and show him their love in their eyes, but never, never, never in loving words. No one would ever be so undignified as to openly discuss his feelings with anyone. So Umialik lay bearing alone the agony of insult, the arrogant self-possession which had been formerly his, now gone.

Umialik grew up as an orphan reared by an old grandmother. The family lived at the end of a long string of dwellings. One year, his parents did not return from a hunting trip and for many years after, his grandmother kept expecting them to return. Early in the morning, while everyone was asleep the grandmother went out to listen. "Maybe my son and daughter-in-law will come this morning and I will not see them coming if I sleep too long." With these words in her heart, she went out of the hut each morning and listened.

Many years she had expected them but they did not come back. She never failed to listen for them each morning. In all kinds of weather, when the sun shone brightly on the snow or in an unbearable blizzard or on a bitterly cold morning, she waited — always going out to look for her loved ones who never came back. In the spring when the summer birds came, she awoke before anyone else and sat many hours listening. She heard the many sounds that the animals and the birds made but never the sound that she knew she would hear if her children were coming.

Like Qayaq's parents, she waited for the return of her dear children. Like Qayaq's parents, she was not blessed with the return of her loved ones. There in front of her hut she made a lonely figure, watching while her grandchild slept in the hut. Her arms in her parka and her hands cupped around her chin, she gazed upon all the many little objects that could be seen.

When she saw smoke curling up from the tops of the other huts, she would give up her vigil, uncover her smoke hole, enter her dwelling and build her fire to prepare food for the day. Many times she picked up her warm little grandchild, put him on her lap, and sat for many hours in sad meditation and longing. No matter how sad she was, the tears refused to flow down her cheeks. She had wept so much that no matter how sad she was, she did not cry anymore.

Their neighbors were always giving them food and skins for clothing. They had no family to look after them, so the neighbors' kindness kept them from want.

The little boy was very intelligent and quick in movement. He was growing more and more aware of his grandmother's sorrow. One early morning, he told his grandmother about what he had seen the night before. "Our little hut lifted itself until I could see far away under it. Many, many animals I saw, and beautiful flowers and leaves waving softly in a gentle wind. Grandmother, what was it that made me see these things?"

"It was your dreams," his grandmother said.

"No, I was not asleep. I was going to ask you if you saw them too, but you were already asleep." He assured his grandmother that what he had seen was not a dream.

"Do not speak of it to anyone," she told him. She knew that her grandchild was inheriting his ancestors' supernatural powers. His young eyes were being opened to be able to look upon things that no ordinary eyes could see.

From time to time, the little hut kept lifting for him but, as he grew older, the beautiful visions were becoming farther apart and instead of beautiful flowers and leaves, he saw objects that travelled in the air without wings.

"Last night I saw a marmot having a quarrel with a raven. Their quarreling turned into a fearsome fight and the black bird was torn to pieces. Still he was struggling for his life although he was in little shreds," the boy reported one morning.

"You have seen two souls of two shamans that are probably enemies," his grandmother said. "When the souls travel at night, they use the garb of the animals that they believe in, or that they claimed to obtain power from." The wise old grandmother had explanations for everything he asked about.

When the boy was old enough to go out to gather wood for their fire, he would come home and tell his grandmother about what he saw. One day he came home and told of a very special experience he had had. "A little weasel came close to me and took his hood off and under his hood was a human head. He said, 'I am one of your ancestors. I have been watching you for some time. I am always thirsty and hungry. When you eat, if you pretend to throw food on the ground, I will eat. When you drink, if you sprinkle some water on the ground, I shall drink. In return, I shall help to make you an Umialik.' Before I could answer, he put his hood on, and a little weasel scampered away."

Then the grandmother explained, "The souls of the dead are all around us and we cannot see them. They are thirsty and hungry. When we sit down to eat our food, if they try to pick some up, it shrinks away from them between their fingers. When they walk along the river flowing with running water and they stoop down to drink, the water shrinks away from them. But when we call on them and say, 'Here is some food for you to eat and here is some water for you to drink,' saying it as if we were really talking to

Spirits at Night
Kenojuak Ashevak

them and seeing them, then they will be able to eat and drink."

The grandmother also explained, "When a child is dressed in the name of a dead relative, the soul of the dead relative has clothes to wear."

Many of the boy's ancestors became known to him in this manner. Many little animals took their hoods off to talk to him. They would say, "If you are in need of help, just think of me, I will be there to help you. Remember me, too, when you sit down to eat and drink."

Day after day, the boy listened to the explanations of his grandmother. Day after day, the grandmother kept thinking about her grandson. Many sleepless nights she spent thinking of her grandson's future and hoping, too, that through him some sign might come from her son and daughter-in-law.

She would say to herself, "Maybe someday he will be powerful enough to find out what has happened to my children."

She hoped that the boy might come home and say, "A little animal came to me today and took his hood off and told me that he was my father." Or he might say, "A little animal came to me today and took her hood off and told me that she was my mother."

These words she longed to hear, hoping that if her son and his wife were not alive then she and her grandson might thus come in contact with their souls. But as the years went by, they were never given a sign to tell them about their loved ones.

In this manner gradually his ancestors took possession of the boy little by little, giving him his supernatural eyesight and guiding him to wisdom through the interpretations of the wise old grandmother.

There was a shaman in this settlement who was kind and had never taken a soul so as to kill anyone. He used his supernatural powers to protect his relatives and was always willing to perform a rite to save a person when he was asked to. To him Umialik's

grandmother went for help after she was sure that
the boy was going to be a man with supernatural
powers. The boy must learn how to use the powers
kindly and wisely.

When she entered the good shaman's big round
dwelling, the family was sitting all around the walls.
A big open fire was blazing in the middle of the room,
its smoke rising straight up through the open skylight.
A man was talking and the men kept laughing at
whatever he said. Gathered here was a very happy
family. The shaman was an old chief that had never
in his life hurt anybody's feelings. His reward for his
good life was having a happy family. His sons and
daughters and their children were all alive. Many of
his family lived with him in his big house and many
dwellings around were filled with his relatives.

The grandmother envied him for this. She had no
relative alive but her grandson. The shamans that were her
ancestors had no descendants for they had taken lives through
their supernatural powers, thinking they were righting a wrong
done to them by some other men. If only these evil shamans had
not tried to avenge themselves, she would have been saved from
days and days of sorrow.

She sat down beside the entrance of the good leader's house
and listened to the story that so amused the men of the household.

When the story was over and all was quiet, the leader said to her,
"I have been expecting you to come to me. I have been watching
your grandson. He will have great supernatural powers. He will
become a shaman. You have endured much grief. And I have
grieved with you for you are not responsible for your sorrows. I
have hoped you might come to see me. I want to thank you for

Big Man
Thomas Sivuraq

Shaman with Bear on Head
Joanasi Naluiyuk

coming to me today. I have looked forward to this privilege for some time."

The old woman could not say a word. She was so overcome by the thought of this man's knowledge of the loss and grief which she thought was known only to her and her grandson.

The shaman's wife followed her out of the house and told her to wait while she went into a cache that was a big dugout covered with sod over the frame. The wife came out with an armful of dried caribou meat and gave it to the old woman. The wife was very pleased to know that the old woman had come to her husband for help. She knew her husband would use his supernatural powers to help the old woman and her grandson. The power of her husband was her happiness. She was a very proud woman — happy, kind, and intelligent.

So her grandchild's boyhood was spent with this kind old shaman. He was taught never to forget any ancestor, not even those who had been long-dead.

The first animal that the boy ever killed was a little ermine or weasel. This was skinned and the meat was left out where it was caught.

At that time, a voice spoke to him, "When you have reached home and sit down to eat, you must say, 'Weasel, you must be my strength and you will always be my charm.' Then you pretend to throw some food and some water on the floor. Say, 'Here, come eat and drink with me.' One of your ancestors used the garb of a weasel to speak to you for the first time. Your grandmother will know what to do with the ermine skin."

The soft white ermine skin was dried and tanned and sewn onto the boy's parka. He had to wear it all the time. If for any reason he did not wear his parka, the grandmother saw to it that the weasel skin was attached to something else he was wearing. Whatever happened, he must always wear the little soft white ermine skin with a little black tip at the end of its tail.

The boy grew and grew. He caught animals for their food and clothing and he and his grandmother no longer needed to depend on the kindness of their neighbors. This was what his grandmother had looked forward to. Each catch she personally took care of willingly and expertly. In time, they became wealthy. Wealth at this time meant furs for clothing and dugouts deep in the permafrost full of food — food that will keep for years, wealth that could be shared with the village.

But some time before this, while the boy was still growing into manhood, there came a certain stormy night. He and his grandmother were eating by the fire that was slowly dying. A seal oil lamp was giving the room a soft hazy light.

The wind was blowing wild outdoors. Now and then a wisp of fine snow came in under the skin that was hung up for the door and which was now raised a little at the bottom to let in some air so the smoke could make its way to the opening at the ceiling without spreading in the room. Their little sod house was warm and cozy. The frame was made of split young trees, covered with sod and coated with hard mud so that not a bit of wind could penetrate.

The roaring of the on-rushing wind and snow made them grateful to be inside a comfortable, cozy *ipnulik* (sod house). No one would want to face the storm now. Its cold was too bitter. Its wind piled up the snowdrifts around the sod house. Only tips of large boulders stood up here and there. Out on the tundra, where the wind in a few places was sweeping away large clouds of snow, single thin strands of grass, their bushy tops bleached and dried to a yellow shade, swayed and turned wildly. On the distant mountainside, spruce trees, though snow and ice encrusted, showed patches of deep winter green.

From the rear of their igloo there was a *"chee-kei-chu-kle-chu ..."*

"What was that?" Startled by the noise, they listened. Then, it came again — *"chee-kei chee-kei chee-kei."* Both were looking at the rear of the sod home when a little weasel appeared. There was no hole through the wall and no hole in the ground. It just appeared so very unexpectedly.

It disappeared for awhile and then it appeared again with — *"Chee-kei, chee-kei."* The two people looked at each other without uttering a word and kept watching it. They sat very still. Standing on its hind legs sniffing in the air — coming down on all fours and then rising onto its hind legs again, it kept looking at them and saying, *"Chee-kei, chee-kei — ."*

Something that was not a little matter was being shown to them. "Isn't he going to take his hood off and let us know what this is all about?" the young man wondered. For what seemed a long time, the little weasel stayed with them but not once did it lift its hood and speak. When finally it left them, the room was cold and the oil in the lamp was almost gone.

The grandson shook his body. "I feel cold," he said. He was trembling all over; his shoulders were lifting with deep hard gasps as if he were fighting to continue breathing. With a whistling and whirring noise as if from many wings, the wind beat upon the little house in the thickness of flying snow all that night.

Sometime in that terrible night of blizzard, the young man cried out, "This room is too small for me. I am going out!"

"No, no, don't go out. Have you gone crazy?" His grandmother shouted.

The young man only uttered words that his grandmother could not understand, saying them fast and loud as if he was very angry at someone. Stamping his feet, he shouted and lowered his big frame, bending his knees and shaking as if trying to shake something off. He went around the fire two times and left.

The grandmother stood looking at the door for awhile, expecting him to come back in, but he did not come back. The young man had left without his outer parka and mittens. The thin caribou skin that was his inside parka next to his skin (with the skin of the ermine sewn to it somewhere) was not enough to keep him warm.

Wishing to inform the wise shaman about the happening in the night and frightened about her grandson, the old woman put on her outer garments and making sure that her hood would not be blown off her head, she started out. As she lifted the door flap, the wind hit her in the face and made her gasp for breath. She could feel the flakes of snow striking her face with sharp little pains as if from many needle points. Her eyes were forced to stay shut. She tried to make a few steps but she felt herself being lifted off her feet. She was forced to sit down. She could not see anything. The wind was whizzing by with an unbearable whipping around her ears. A few yards away was her nearest neighbor. She must reach her neighbor's house before she was numb with cold. Her neighbor would send somebody to the wise shaman for her. Maybe the wise shaman could do something to stop this terrible storm, too.

She crawled along, feeling her way with her hands and knees. It seemed to her that she should be almost to the neighbor's sod house. She thought it was very slow and hard to get anywhere when she was on her hands and knees. Crawling and clinging to the hard snow under her, she at last touched something that felt like the flap of a door and lifting it she crawled through. Then pushing up the ruff of her hood, she opened her eyes. Nobody was in this sod house, just a few coals of fire and a lamp that was almost out of oil. Why … why she was in her own sod house! Her stone lamp was almost out of seal oil! A little flame no bigger than a salmon-berry was struggling to stay alive!

Instead of going ahead to the neighbor's, she had turned about somewhere and backtracked herself. No wonder it seemed a long time for her to get anywhere. She was almost to the neighbor's and had turned back.

She put wood on the fire and out of the wooden bucket of seal oil got oil to fill the stone lamp. Then she pulled up the moss wick for the flame with a sharp stick. And once again, the little sod house had light and warmth.

Leaving her home again, she felt sure that this time she was not going to turn around again. She gritted her teeth hard and though the wind took the breath out of her, she kept crawling on her hands and knees, clinging to the hard snow in an effort not to be lifted by the wind. Her hood's ruff hanging down in front of her face made it feel wet and sticky. Thick clouds of flying snow and roaring wild wind beat hard against her. Little by little she made her way. Her hands feeling their way in the snow were becoming numb with cold. Her fur mittens that were always so warm could not, this night, keep out the cold. Finally, she felt something give under her touch. It was the door flap of a sod house. She found the bottom edge and lifting it, she crawled through. Raising the ruff of her hood, she opened her eyes. In the glow of an oil lamp, she saw the few coals of a fire! She was in her own home again!

A second time she put wood on the fire and out of the wooden bucket got seal oil to fill the stone lamp. A second time she pulled up the moss wick for the flame with a sharp stick. And once again the little sod house had light and warmth.

She felt alone, all alone, in this great wilderness. The sod house seemed to have an emptiness that reached beyond its roof, beyond the roaring wind — almost touching the far away stars. Her neighbors were so very near to her. When it was not stormy, they were very close, indeed, just a few yards away. Still tonight she had not been able to reach them. Now she wished that she was sitting inside the door flap of her neighbor's house, hearing the grandfather's stories — or better still, sitting inside the door flap of the shaman's house, hearing his voice give her words of wisdom and understanding.

Where was her grandson? What made him go out in this storm? Had he gone crazy? Had the souls of his ancestors taken possession of his body? If they had, perhaps they would take care of him, he who had been especially instructed by them to be one of those to give them food and water.

As she sat thinking, a little weasel appeared. She was startled. Did the little weasel, her grandson's helping spirit, come to warn her about what was to happen?

"*Chee-kei, chee-kei.*" There was no hole in the wall and no hole in the ground. The little weasel just appeared again unexpectedly.

It disappeared for a while and then it appeared again with "*Chee-kei, chee-kei.*" The old woman sat very still — watching it. Standing on its hind legs sniffing in the air, coming down on all four feet, and then rising up on its hind legs again, the weasel kept looking at her and saying, "*Chee-kei, chee-kei.*"

The old woman knew that something that was not a little matter was being shown to her! Wasn't he going to take his hood off and let her know what this was all about?

For a long time the little weasel stayed with her but not once did he lift his hood and speak.

The weasel had come to tell her to do something, but what? Finally she remembered the offerings that her grandson was told to make to the souls of the ancestors. She picked up some food and sprinkled it over the room, and she poured water over the ground of the sod house floor. In her eagerness, she forgot that she was just to sprinkle a little. All around the fire now briskly burning she threw dry food and poured fresh water, chanting, "Here come, all of you people that are my ancestors, come eat and drink. Please, please bring my boy back to me. I want him back and please, don't let anything hurt him!"

She went around the fire once more, but then everything looked as if it were revolving around her. For a while she saw the interior of the sod house dimly, then more and more of it became blotted out, until blackness was all around her. The roaring of the wind outdoors made her head ache and she became unconscious.

When she opened her eyes, the room was cold. The fire had gone out, and the little flame in the lamp was flickering in an attempt to give light to the little house, which now no longer needed it, for streaks of dawn were streaming into the house from the skylight. The flames on the lamp wick were far apart now, and in the morning light she could see entwined in the sod little cranberry bushes and tiny herbs hanging down a few inches from the walls and ceiling.

All was quiet and she moved her cramped old limbs with an effort. She felt tired. Her grandson was not home yet.

She went out of the house. The sun was just coming up over the horizon, shining on fields and fields of wavy, bluish and pinkish hard snow. Her neighbor's igloo was so near, though she could not reach it in the storm and darkness of last night. Smoke was peacefully curling out of the opening on its roof.

Over the hard and noisily crunching snow, she made her way to the wise shaman's house. When she entered everyone was eating. The wise shaman, stripped to the waist in his warm house, was sitting next to the fire.

As she sat down by the door flap, he gave her a smile and said, "I have been expecting you. You slept long this morning. I think this

L E L A   K I A N A   O M A N

is one of the very few times the sun got up before you did."

He was a happy, poised person. Although he was older than his visitor by many years, he looked much younger. The hair at his temples was just beginning to gray, but an untrimmed mustache on his upper lip was all black. When he spoke, he showed two rows of even white teeth which, when he smiled, were seen to be only slightly worn down. His friendly brown eyes, surrounded by many wrinkles when he smiled, were gazing at his visitor sympathetically.

His visitor could not lift up her eyes to meet his eyes but kept looking on the floor, bare ground covered with fine willow boughs.

The mistress of the house stood up and taking a wooden plate full of food set it before her. She did not want to eat. How could she? Her throat was a hard dry knot that refused to be swallowed down.

The wise shaman, the Umialik of the village, spoke comforting words, "Do not worry too much. Have faith in the souls of your ancestors. I am sure your grandson will come back to you. I saw what had happened. I tried to warn you, but you could not understand the meaning. I made you see the weasel. Through him, I tried to tell you everything would be all right, but I only frightened you each time I showed him to you. Since the weasel was your grandson's good luck animal, through it I tried to make you see that everything would be all right.

"Your grandson is being put to the test. His supernatural eyesight must be tested. You must not worry too much about his body. Don't you know the soul is immortal? Whatever happens to the body, the soul goes on to be something or someone else. I saw him flying out of your igloo and shouting like a happy child. He raced with the wind. Reaching the mountain, he skimmed over it. You tried to come to tell me about it, but I already knew what had happened. So I made you turn back to your home each time you made an effort to come out in the storm.

"I am very sorry you are made to suffer. Someone has to suffer when someone makes a mistake. Your forefathers were powerful. Jealousy and greed and vengeance compelled them to take lives of other people. Wrong already done will not be righted by another wrong. My shaman-ancestors were like me. They used their supernatural powers kindly and wisely. I am sure my path of peace was paved for me by them before I took powers from their souls."

The old grandmother who seemed to be so very wise was years and years behind the shaman in wisdom. There she sat not eating at all now. Try as she might, she knew that she could not eat.

"My wife will stay with you until your grandson comes home. He may come back today and he may be away for many days. You need not worry anymore. If the souls of the ancestors could not take good care of him, they would not have taken possession of his body," said the kind old shaman.

The shaman's wife went home with the old woman. All that day they sat with a fire between them, splitting and twisting sinew for thread. From time to time, one of them would add more wood to the fire and always they talked to each other.

When the night came, the wind was blowing softly. It made a fluttering noise up at the skylight. Then a soft whispering sound was heard by the two old women as they listened for the boy, between their murmurings to each other. The grandmother was very glad that she did not have to spend this night alone. The room looked friendly now, the soft glow from the lamp and the flames of the fire gave it a bright warm light.

Early in the morning on the fifth day, the boy came. He lifted the skin that was their door and he came in. He looked as if he were just coming in from the next sod house. He was dressed just as he had been when he rushed out into the blizzard. He made his way to his bedding and sat down. His face was pale and he looked very weak.

The two old women who had just had their breakfast pretended they were not surprised by his coming.

"Give me some water. I am very thirsty," he said. His grandmother gave it to him without a word and then sat down at her place again. The two women watched him as he lay down on his bedding. Evenly breathing and sometimes snoring a little, he was soon sound asleep.

"I had better go home now. I am so happy for you. I am so happy that the boy is back," the guest said. The grandmother thanked her for staying with her.

The boy rested for many days and did not explain his absence. His grandmother did not ask him where he had been although she was very curious to know.

Early one morning, the kind old shaman sent for the young man and told him it was about time they go hunting again.

From time to time the young man would go away with the wise shaman. Each time he would see more of the things that could be seen only through eyes that had supernatural powers. Finally, he was not possessed bodily any more. He was strong enough to control his own body, but his soul travelled at night leaving his body behind quite lifeless.

By now he was almost a full-fledged shaman, ready to be called Umialik. "Through me, my shaman ancestors drink and eat again," he would say.

By now the grandmother was certain that he would find news of his lost parents, but he never said anything about them. What had happened to them? If they were alive they would come home, surely. If they were dead, their souls would become known to them through him. Or was it that they did not possess supernatural powers? That they had dissolved into nothing? If they had not, what happened to them, and where did they go?

When a loved one dies or is lost, he or she comes back in many

Animals Disguising as People
Marion Tuu'luuq

different ways. Some are born as a baby and some are made known through animals or in dreams that they are around again.

One day the sun was very hot. Umialik and the young man were hunting caribou. From the distance they saw a herd. The caribou being so wild had been aware of the hunters before the hunters saw the caribou. The two men could see them far away, running in a different direction. The younger man wanted to chase them and see if he could spear them. The older man protested but he could not do anything to stop him. "Don't you see they are too far away? On your way back home, the night will overtake you. In your position the night should not overtake you. You must be very careful for you are not an ordinary man." Saying thus, the shaman begged him not to go. The younger man felt it was very thrilling to be running after the caribou. He refused to think about what should happen to him on his way home in the dark.

Stripped to his waist and a spear in one hand he gave chase to the caribou. The older man picked his clothes up and started for home after watching the young man speeding on over the tundra, never for a moment slackening his pace no matter what was underfoot. The old shaman took his clothes home to his grandmother and told her not to expect him home for some time. "I cannot tell you how many days he will be away this time."

Catching up with the herd of caribou, the young man speared and killed one. As he stopped to pull the spear out of the already dead animal, the herd ran many miles away. Spear in hand, he sped on after them. He caught up with them again, killing one, and again gave chase. Thinking that he had enough to keep himself busy for the day, he stopped, and getting his knife out, he dressed the last kill.

He hung the meat on nearby young trees and left it. He would come back for it later. Going on to the next kill, he skimmed lightly over the rocks. All alone now, there was nothing to deter him. Any kind of surface was no obstacle to his young energetic body. Finishing the last catch, he was taking his time. He knew the night would overtake him before he was even half-way home but he did not care.

On the way he had to pass a very high cliff. A cliff with a grey smooth rock for a wall, shooting straight to the depths of the very wide and deep river. He would have to walk past this and over the long ridge it made. A few miles from this he noticed that it was dusk already. "Funny, I should think it would be mid-afternoon now," he said to himself.

As he walked, he also noticed he was lifted off the ground. He felt that he was walking on hard ground. Still he saw his feet moving in the air above the ground. He turned around and retraced his steps. Reaching the ground, he made sure his soles were flat on the ground before he started walking again. "My feet better stay on the ground this time," he thought to himself. A few steps onward he found himself walking the air again! Turning around, he again was on the ground. Moving away, he walked slowly and carefully, but to his horror he was in the air again. Plain thin air felt like hard steady ground. Still he saw his feet elevated from the ground. He retraced his steps a third time and sat down. "Maybe sitting a while will break the spell," he said to himself.

He stood up to begin his journey and a few steps away he was in the air again!

"I would like to reach my grandmother, she will worry about me again. Someone playing a trick on me must be sure I will be cared for." Thinking in this way, he went ahead.

He knew he was facing home and the cliff loomed not very far ahead of him. At a certain height he was walking on level ground. When the night came, he knew it would be very black. Night fell without a moon, and the snow was murky black. The thought of walking through the air did not reassure him.

Ahead of him, he saw two runners. He felt suddenly glad that the shaman had sent him help. But, oddly enough, their feet did not touch the ground either! When the runners reached him, he did not recognize them. They did not look like anyone he knew.

"We've come to take you home. You have no cause to be afraid, everything will be all right," said one of the runners. The young man could not answer, he was not given any choice. He was not going to be responsible for what should happen.

The young future chief saw many hills and ponds racing by under them. Finally they were almost at the bottom of the cliff. The two messengers led him straight to the face of the hideous cliff. This grey wall of flat smooth rock opened to let them in. The two young men sat down and took their places among many people sitting against the walls in a half circle. The young man was left standing in the middle of the room. The room, the interior of the cliff, which had looked like a solid rock, was very brightly lit with beams of light that seemed to come from nowhere.

Women, children, and old men were all staring at him with their shining eyes. He had never seen them before. Not a single person he knew was among them.

"We are so very happy to be able to come in contact with you. We have been watching you taking strength from your ancestors, and also know through you that they eat and drink again.

"When you have plenty to eat, and the food is easy for you to catch, we suffer from hunger. When you happen to catch plenty, we wish that you would leave a little at this place. A little tiny piece of meat will multiply into many in our sight. We also are very fond

LELA KIANA OMAN

of wolverine skins. A little strip of wolverine will multiply into many skins in our sight."

An old man sitting at the rear of the room was talking to him. The young man, the future Umialik, stripped to the waist, spear in one hand, was led out. He was not given a chance to speak and he did not touch anything. The same young men that brought him in led him out and walked with him until he touched the ground again. When they left him, the sun was coming up from behind a mountain in the east. "Early morning, so soon!" He said to himself.

He reached home and found his grandmother sitting in the sod house having her breakfast.

After sitting down on his bed-clothing, he said, "Give me some water, I am very thirsty." After a drink, he stretched his big body and lay down. Soon he was fast asleep.

The grandmother said nothing, only glad that five days of worrying over her beloved child were over once more. Five days he was away, to him just one short night, spent as the invited guest of the *Iqsingat*.

After this, he became wealthy. He had a new stone house surrounded by many storage caches, some dug into the frost in the ground, some perched high on stilts. (How he became the owner of this house is not told.) His grandmother was becoming very feeble and old and was not strong enough any more to take care of his caches.

Seeing this, the kind old shaman suggested the young man take one of his granddaughters for his wife. Now the old grandmother had someone to take care of her in her last days. Becoming so very old, she was continuously whining about her son and daughter-in-law. "Why couldn't my grandchild find ways to find out something about his parents' disappearance? Isn't he strong enough in his supernatural powers to satisfy me of the most desirable thing in my life?"

The old woman was insistent because she knew that she had not long to live. Quietly and patiently, the girl waited on her, making things comfortable as best as she could. But the cackling voice of the old woman, who could not shed any tears, found many things to whine about. Every day she made a remark about her disappointment, whispering to herself now and then. In her very last days, the grandchildren did not sleep at night. She was sick and was demanding constant attention from them. Finally and at last, she was quiet, not saying a word. Just taking a few hard wheezing breaths, she died.

She had known sorrow that she had no escape from, the sorrow that someone must endure because her ancestors were powerful shamans and took lives to satisfy their greedy nature. Being a descendant of these evil ones, she had to suffer for the mistakes they made.

Not long after she died, the girl's grandfather, the kind old shaman, died too, leaving them bewildered, not knowing what to do. The people of the village had to look upon the young shaman as a possible leader. "The old Umialik taught you about many things. Perhaps his soul will come to you and give you more power," they told him.

From then on the young shaman became an Umialik. He was a rich man now with a nice young wife that worshipped the very ground he walked on. But Fate did not smile upon him with kindness. His wife died at childbirth, leaving him broken-hearted. With no one to breast-feed her, the child had to be sacrificed.

He took another young woman for a wife and she too died, leaving him a baby girl, a beautiful little girl that later became Qayaq's wife. A mere female — not a son to take over and carry on when he passed away.

He saw visions at night. Like every shaman he was able to have

LELA KIANA OMAN

visions. Many nights his igloo raised itself a few feet off the ground for him. Many evil shamans, garbed as the animals they believed in, travelled at night. Or their souls, just as they really are, came to him, looking like their bodies that they left at home quite lifeless. The body, he knew, could not live when the soul left it.

He could not defend his own as the kind old shaman did, who had taught him so many things and tried to teach him how to use his power kindly and wisely. Many, many times the old shaman warned him not to hurt anybody's feelings. "What ever happens do not fight back, it does not pay. You will only make worse what is bad." These words, for him, were hard to fulfill. His two wives' deaths were hard to take without fighting back. So he began taking lives. Perhaps making somebody suffer, he would feel better.

The only child, who turned out to be a girl, dared to live. To him she only looked like a mockery. If she were a boy, she would have died, too. She had survived his ill treatment so far. He could not kill her with his own hands. The love of a father outweighed his bitterness.

But despite his affection for his daughter, he could not bear to see her happy, so after choosing husbands for her, he killed them off. The Umialik made her husbands suffer by taking their lives. He thought this would give him pleasure. But the old shaman had been right, taking lives only increased the pain.

Descendants of the people who traced their ancestry to Tulugak's (the Raven Man's) clan, lived in this shaman who became Umialik, through whom the souls of the past great shamans drank and ate again. *Iqsingat* came in contact with the living through him. But now he was a very bitter and treacherous father-in-law and an unhappy Umialik.

He became very well-to-do and was now the owner of a huge stone house.*

*The domelike round-shaped Umialik's house is in the story. Where and how he became the owner is not told. These large round houses — bigger than the other dwellings of the village — are often mentioned as being homes of the strong.

For many days after the battle with the one-footed bird, Qayaq and his father-in-law hunted together again. But soon Qayaq was beginning to be very restless.

Spring was in the air, the evergreen trees were dripping with melting snow, many tussocks on the tundra were bare and the snow had flat thin icy patches on it all over the side of the mountain. Qayaq walked up the mountain by himself. Half-way up he saw many ptarmigans on the wing, and some landed on the slope above him. As he neared them, they turned into many men and women. They had landed there to spend the night, so Qayaq stopped to spend the night with them. He had almost nothing with him. He had left most of his things with his wife. All that he had with him were the stone knife that he had used to kill the one-footed bird, and a bit of the *akutuq* his mother had made for him, which he carried in a container that was the stomach of an animal.

He knew that the people he was to stop with were really ptarmigans. But now they seemed to be many men and women making ready to go to bed. Qayaq had no bedding, while the others had caribou skins for their bedding. Seeing this, they gave him one black caribou skin for a mattress and a white one for a blanket. Between these warm skins, he was very comfortable and fell asleep instantly.

The next day Qayaq awoke suddenly. The sun was already coming up over the mountain giving warmth to his body and everything seemed to be dripping with melting snow. Still, he felt cold and uncomfortable. Where were his caribou mattress and blanket? There on top of him was a little slim white feather from a ptarmigan's tail — he sat up and under him was a black shiny long feather, also from a ptarmigan's tail. He was all alone now. The men and women, his companions of last night, were gone.

When he reached the top of the high mountain, he looked all

around him. He was somewhere near the head of Noatak River. He made up his mind that he was going to stick close to the river as best he could. From the top of the mountain he saw in the distance another mountain. At the bottom he could see a herd of caribou. In order to catch them he had to cross the big flat. He had no desire to kill them, so he made his way down the side of the mountain slowly. The slope was covered with patches of trees here and there. When he was in among the trees, he could not see the herd of caribou. Standing in the open valley they were in plain view. Walking through the trees, he made his way to the bottom. The flat was covered with patches of snow here and there. If the tundra had been thawed, it would have been swampy all over: soft-sinking sod, little blades of grass here and there, all kinds of moss now sticking up like little animals half hidden. The going was easy with icy hard sod underfoot.

Sunrise of Tanaqaaq
Malaya Akulukjuk

The caribou noticed him when he was halfway across. In alarm, they swiftly ran up the mountain to escape him. Their heavy antlers, thrown back above their sleek bodies, were carried by long, limber and swift legs, as they climbed up to the top of the mountain. At the top, they stood looking down at him. Qayaq did not change his pace, he had no desire to kill them. He had no spear in hand, only a stone knife hanging down from his belt. In a moment, the herd was not visible to him any more. When he reached the top, he saw the caribou had changed their course and were travelling west following the range of high mountains. Without changing his pace, he followed them. After passing a few mountains, he was coming around a bend at the bottom into the little valley.

To his surprise, the caribou had stopped here and were waiting for him. They looked beautiful, their heads held high and very grandly, with unblinking, large black eyes. Qayaq stood for a moment very puzzled and when they failed to move he approached them. One of the largest came forward to meet him. Stopping a few feet away, the caribou bent down and bumped the ground with his nose several times, causing his fur hood to peel back from a human head.

"Do you wish to become one of us?" he asked Qayaq. Qayaq thought it would be fun to be one of them for a time.

"I would like to become one of you. I think it would be wonderful," Qayaq answered sincerely.

"It is not thrilling to be a caribou. You see we are hunted for food by many animals and men. We are on the alert always," the caribou man cautioned him.

"If I may, I would like to become one of you and go wherever you go. I do not care what happens to me." Knowing that his soul could never die, Qayaq begged.

"All right then, don't ever say that I did not warn you," the caribou man said. Calling forward one of the other caribou and taking an extra skin from him, he covered Qayaq with it. Qayaq stood on four legs feeling very strong and light. He knew just how he looked now. Beautiful greying fur covered him, for it was spring, close to shedding time. He felt free and happy.

"When we are aware of strangers, we run as fast as we can. Be always ready to run for your life," the caribou man said, pulling his hood forward again. "When you start, you must always keep your eyes on the distant horizon. If you do not, you will not keep up with us. You will be stumbling on everything in your path. This you must never forget."

With these words Qayaq was initiated into the herd of caribou who lived at the head of Noatak river. He spent the springtime living free of care, roaming everywhere with the herd of caribou.

As he roamed, he ate many strange things that he was not used to. As a human, Qayaq loved foods like *muktuk* (whale skin), berries, all kinds of meat, whale meat and oil. Because he was used to these, how could the tundra moss seem to be such tasty food? Or was the leader of the herd making things look good to him so he would not be discouraged? He did not know.

One hot afternoon he was resting on the ground. All at once the herd jumped on their feet and thundered past him. He knew they were startled by a prowler, and he stood up quickly and tried to run. He stumbled over a stone and landed on his chest with a bang, jarring every bone in his enormous body. On his feet again, he made an effort but he was lurching sideways, offbalance, and in a few yards he tripped and rolled over on his back. "This will never do," he thought to himself. Taking his time, even though his great heart was pounding with fright, he stood on his legs again, and he caught up with the others although they were already a long way ahead.

Qayaq the caribou dared not look back, every minute expecting to feel the teeth of some animal at his hind legs or the spear or arrow of a man piercing his body. How well he knew the sending of these sharp weapons! Now the idea of being a possible target was no comfort to his shaking body and pounding heart. So far he was not feeling pain in his body. Somehow and at last he caught up with the others, who were all standing, watching his approach. The leader met him and reproached him for forgetting his instructions.

Sudden Movement
Geela Akulukjuk

Running Caribou
Helen Kalvak

"Don't you know you can never run if you do not keep your eyes on the distant horizon? I told you never to forget that. If that wolf had made up his mind to catch one of us, you would be dead now!" the lead caribou said.

"Oh, so that was what we got away from." Qayaq was very glad that the wolf did not give chase. "Next time I'll try and remember to keep my eyes on the distant horizon."

Not long after this incident, the caribou heard in the distance a rattling noise. It came from far away — probably from over the mountain — but they heard it. Somebody was walking and was making all sorts of noise. Distant squeaking and rustling noises he made, and they heard it as if it was banging against their ears.

Qayaq's companions were startled. Jumping to their feet, they thundered past him. He, too, stood up and this time he was not going to forget! He saw blue sky and puffy clouds scattered above the surface of the rosy world, made rosy by the sun that was already riding high over the mountain. He ran as fast as his four untrained legs could carry him. When he noticed the thundering around him had ceased, he stopped. Oops, he was among them! Not so complicated after all! He knew they were a distance away from the intruder.

"A man this time," their leader said.

"Why was he so very noisy?" Qayaq was very curious.

"That was a lazy man; never in his life has he arisen from bed before sun-up. That is why he walks noisily, his clothes rattling and echoing all over the hills. He does not know that it is because he is so lazy that he walks so noisily."

Once more, many days later, the caribou were being approached by a man who was a great hunter. They were not aware of him until he was close. Suddenly, a man with spear in hand was swiftly running in their direction. They were getting up to run, but the earth tilted in their sight, toward the man. Qayaq saw the flat surface of the tundra looking like a slope of a mountain. What was this? Instead of running up the slope, they sped down towards the man. As he ran, Qayaq saw they were being forced to run in a circle a mile wide around the hunter. Seeing this, the man began to shout at them, standing still now. Waving his arms, stripped to the waist, he was whistling and shouting at them. Hearing this, the ground tilted more until Qayaq, feeling dizzy, thought that he could easily roll down to the man! The herd was now less than a quarter of a mile from him, still racing in single file. Qayaq heard his companions snorting to themselves as they sped around in a circle closing in on the hunter. The horizon passed swiftly. Their heads high, antlers thrown back over their shoulders, the bodies close to the sloping ground and hoofs pointing toward the man, in their panic they made bits of tundra fly.

Now within range for his spear, the man made his kill. In a circle that looked like a swirling smooth rope they raced, still drawn to the man who was not shouting at them now. Busy with the killing, he did not have time to shout and whistle now. Terrifyingly close, Qayaq saw the hunter raise his spear in the air and point it in his direction, but Qayaq was not touched. Another caribou, running a little before him, went down with a crash, almost touching him with his hoofs. Qayaq leaped over the fallen caribou, never for a moment taking his eyes away from the now blurry, swirling horizon. The ground had tilted and it looked as if they were going to be thrown in a heaving pile on top of the man.*

Finally and at last, the earth righted itself. The big tundra became flat. Easily and swiftly they moved away from the hunter who had killed many of their companions. Not very far away they stopped,

*Lela says, "Many years ago expert hunters had the ability to use their powers with the caribou in this way." [The Editors]

panting, tongues hanging out and they looked back at the man, now sitting down resting.

Not long after this terrifying experience, Qayaq became a human being again ...

Qayaq walked and walked.

He continued his travelling among many mountains. A few days of travelling found him meeting a man. The stranger was very friendly. Seeing that Qayaq was alone and had nothing besides the stone knife hanging down from his belt, he tried to make him go back where he came from.

"Over the mountain and across a flat there are many people," the stranger warned. "They are my people, no stranger can ever come near us. No stranger has a chance to be among us. He is always killed by the three leaders that control the whole community. I have never seen anyone survive after they set their eyes on him."

"Please let me go with you," Qayaq said. "I am not afraid. Only let me see what they look like." Qayaq's heart was already pounding with excitement. Thrilled to think a possible danger was near at hand, he begged to be led to the man's people. The man could not discourage him, so he led him up the mountain.

When they reached a point halfway between the mountain and the settlement, they saw two runners coming to meet them. They had already known they were to be visited. Without seeing Qayaq, they knew that he was coming.

The men ran toward Qayaq and his host. They were tall and had an appearance of strength. Broad husky brutes, they were.

Qayaq gazed upon them and he decided the men were not to be trifled with, so he dug out his pouch of *akutuq*, took a little on his

LELA KIANA OMAN

fingertip, and licked it. It seemed to him every time he took a taste, it was growing more appetizing.

"Why don't you turn back or make for cover while you still have a little chance! You're a fine young man, I'd hate to see you getting killed." The stranger was very concerned about him.

"Don't worry about me. I have never turned anybody down from asking for an excitement," said Qayaq.

"If ever you manage to reach the settlement, I want you to be my guest," the stranger said.

"I will be very proud to be your guest. I thank you very much. Don't think for a moment that I will not be your guest." Qayaq was so very sure of himself. And why not? "The blood I shed into this *akutuq* will be your youth and your strength," his mother had told him.

He and the kind man were coming down to meet the speeding runners. When Qayaq was within range of the arrows, one of the runners stopped and let an arrow fly straight at Qayaq. Qayaq easily stepped aside, caught it in his hand and broke it in two. Seeing this, the two let many arrows fly, in quick movements reaching over their shoulders from their arrow bags. Side-stepping swiftly and lightly, Qayaq was catching every arrow. Laughing a little to himself. Very funny! The brutes were going to shoot and kill him.

The flying arrows were coming thicker and thicker and Qayaq, dodging some of them, was catching them right and left, crazily doing a mad dance. Dodging one, catching another, bending his agile body this way and that way, the very idea of this mad dance was so funny to him. He laughed out loud, making his attackers very angry. Very angry indeed! Was someone going to make fools of them? The idea alone was maddening to these people, who wanted their settlement to be safe from others. Finally, the mad dance was over. The two men had run out of arrows.

"You go and meet them. I will see you later," Qayaq said to the friendly stranger, and he ran to the top of the mountain. He had other plans in his mind.

On top of the mountain again, he watched the three men walking back to the settlement, which was on the bank of the Noatak River. Many sod homes surrounded a *qazgi* (a community meeting place), which was a very large structure dwarfing the rest. Lying flat on the ground, he watched to see what actions the people would take next. He saw what was going on among the inhabitants as he gazed upon the settlement with eyes that penetrate and could look into one's soul.

The news spread very quickly, and everyone in the settlement heard about a man who was very brave and survived a rain of arrows. The arrows alone baffled Qayaq. These men had bows and arrows.

The sun was setting as he watched smoke coming out of the tops of many sod homes. The sky above was very blue and everywhere he looked spelled peace. But in that settlement, he saw wrath in the set of every man's lips. They all wondered why he hadn't been killed.

The people of the settlement spoke of Qayaq: "He was not killed by arrows that were sent to him as thick as rain. For once we have run across a human being that is quick in movement and of great strength. Somehow we must catch him." And into their *qazgi* they were gathering. Qayaq saw everyone enter the large structure, every man, woman and child of the village.

Night was coming on now. Infinity showed few stars. Qayaq had to strain his eyes to see the people, for it was dusk. He must somehow cross the open area to get to the *qazgi*. He knew he could not cross the tundra as a man; he had to become something else. He must leave his body here and become something that could

L E L A   K I A N A   O M A N

move silently. The people he was watching appeared to him to be powerful, cunning and intelligent, and they had weapons — weapons he thought that the Umialik's community alone had.

He was wishing very hard to become something else. For once he could not make up his mind what he should become. He was so very absorbed in his thoughts that he did not notice what was happening. The only thing he knew was that he was going in and out of the ground. Solid ground which was at the top of the mountain that was worn down by rains and the wind, he was diving into it like he was in the water.

Qayaq felt very light and small. Puzzled by this, he looked back over his body; little tiny ridges met his eyes, his back was brown and the underside of him was white and at the end of his tail was a black tip. He was squealing, screeching like a weasel at a big frame of a man lying flat on his belly. When his screeching failed to arouse the man, he scrambled on four short legs over to him. The man was not breathing although his eyes were wide open. This was his own body.

When Qayaq became a pike and a caribou he had changed bodily. This time he knew his soul had left his human body and was now weaving easily in and out of tiny burrows in the hard rocky ground as a little weasel. So as a weasel he made his way across the distance between the mountain and the village. Swiftly and quietly he reached the big *qazgi,* and scurried up onto its muddy dome. Reaching the skylight, he lifted one corner of a square covering and peeked in. The room was lit up very brightly by four oil lamps. All around the round interior of the structure he saw many men, women and children, and at the rear were the two men who had made him dance madly among flying arrows. They looked around proudly and sat erect looking very fierce.

A platform wide enough for a man to squat on was built all

around the room. A little above the two fierce bowmen was another man, larger and stripped to the waist. He was a giant, bulging with muscles. Ugly, a scowl on his face, he was not pleased by his subordinates' failure to kill the stranger.

"Of all the ridiculous things I have every heard of, this is the most unforgivable! My two braves let arrows fly like rain and the unknown man survived! For the first time there is someone we have failed to kill. Could my power have gotten away from me? Don't think for a moment that it will not come back. We must keep this village to ourselves. An outsider must never live to spend a night among us," the giant said. Murmurs of agreement went all around the large hall. The giant sat down after his speech, waving his arms and stamping his big feet.

"So, so, no one can ever spend a night among you! You must think you are supreme, superior to all creations! We shall see, we shall see!" Qayaq thought to himself. Then, in his weasel shape, he turned outraged somersaults on top of the big structure near the skylight. Suddenly the little weasel turned into a little fluff of down.

"Ah, ah, he is coming down! Ah, ah." Everyone was straining his eyes watching a little fluff of down drifting down from the skylight! The three nobles were petrified as they sat, their eyes glued on the little fluff of down drifting down unsteadily into their midst. This was so unusual that they knew that it was not an ordinary fluff of down. All was quiet, everybody was shocked to speechlessness as they stared at the fluff of down, tiny and unsteadily making straight for their floor.

Right there in front of their eyes, the down changed. A large man materialized and was looking fiercely eye to eye, looking this way and that way. Qayaq glared at the three large men, the heroes and protectors of the community. Their wrath he saw, as he gazed upon them with eyes that could look into their souls.

One of the three men stood up and approached Qayaq. "How very extraordinary you are. You will not use the doorway to enter!" he said and grabbed him with a firm grip that seemed to dig into Qayaq's shoulders. He almost winced with pain.

"On your knees, on your knees," someone shouted at them. On their knees in a wrestling posture, they held each other, arms around each other. In the grip of his opponent, Qayaq felt that his breath was being squeezed out of his lungs. But he in return tightened his arms around the big brute, and hearing his intake of breath, he knew that his opponent was struggling for breath, too!

Seeing this, the giant and his pal, the second bowman, stood up. "Let's kill him, let's kill him!" they shouted. At this Qayaq's anger mounted higher, until he thought he would go wild with rage.

"No, no, give the stranger a fair chance! I am ashamed of you two. Three are too many against one!" an elderly voice shouted at them. This criticism from an elder made them so angry, and at the same time so humiliated, that all they could do was fume and grunt in their displeasure. They were not acting as they pleased for once. Somehow they were rooted where they sat. The elder who had dared to speak so critically would have to be taken care of later. They made sure of his identity.

Qayaq felt himself being thrown into the air and as he landed on the smooth hard floor. Every bone in his body felt jarred. His ears were ringing crazily and, blending with it, he heard a song. The image of his father as he sang the song came to his mind. His father's magic song gave him a renewed strength. With a terrible grip on his opponent, he jerked him skyward. To his surprise he saw the big brute being thrown into the air, and with superhuman strength, Qayaq jerked him down toward the floor. There was a sickening crash and the man flattened out quite lifeless.

The second bowman approached Qayaq, but the outspoken elder

stood up quickly and pushed his way to the middle of the room. "No fair, no fair! Why not give the stranger time to rest. Can't you see he is still out of breath?" the elder said.

A man in the crowd muttered, "That same man shooting off his mouth again. Tomorrow, by this time, see if he will be living." He glanced at the elderly man irritably.

The elderly speaker was not heeded this time, and the second bowman edged forward. On his feet, he grabbed for the panting Qayaq. "On your knees, on your knees!" Someone was clamoring to be a referee but he was not heeded. The second bowman would not wait, nor would he fall to his knees.

Still Qayaq had time to stagger to his feet. With one hand on Qayaq's shoulder, the bowman made a terrific blow land on his chin, which made Qayaq reel and stagger backwards. Somehow he managed to stay on his two feet. The big brute was approaching with his two fists doubled up. Qayaq waited for him, and as he raised his right fist for a blow, Qayaq ducked under it, making it miss him by a hair's breadth. He heard it make a whizzing noise over his head. The force of the blow sent the big man forward, slightly leaning over. In a split second, Qayaq saw him poised in the air with feet partially off the ground. Seeing his chance Qayaq lunged for the big man's lifted feet and jerking them down with a quick and powerful movement, he made the man land on his chin with a painful slam.

Qayaq's opponent trembled all over and, with eyes staring at nothing, he rolled over on his back and drew his last breath without uttering a sound.

"That was a quick one. Nothing to it at all," Qayaq thought to himself. He knew the man had died, his neck having been broken.

"I'll give it to you! I'll give it to you!" the giant, the only one left of the trio of brutes thundered at Qayaq. There, poised in the air, he stood with bow and arrow — already aiming at Qayaq.

"Don't make a fool out of yourself, you coward," the elderly man in the crowd again spoke, daring to sneer at the giant this time. "You have terrorized this community long enough. Your only hope lies in killing the stranger with your bare hands."

With the weapon still poised in the air, the arrogant giant looked around at the faces. On their many faces he saw a quiet contempt for him. He understood that the odds were against him. If he killed the stranger with a weapon, he would surely lose his standing in the community. If so, he would not be permitted to live — he had made many suffer in the great hall where his brothers carried out his wishes. He understood that the people at last were challenging him. Many young men had been talked into fearing him by their elders. The older men were now clamoring for him to show his strength by killing Qayaq with his bare hands. This argument favoured Qayaq — giving him time to regain his even breathing and prepare himself for another struggle. The two men flat on the floor looked like death to the third brute. He was now given no alternative but to carry on the fight himself.

His face red with rage and with a rumbling noise in his throat, he stood up from his seat and made his way to the middle of the room. A giant of all giants, he was about the largest man Qayaq had ever taken on. A head taller than Qayaq, he scowled down at him. Qayaq would not take his eyes away from the angry face. The giant's ugly, red, and massive face showed that he was not pleased by the sneering contempt of the crowd.

The enraged giant grabbed for Qayaq, but Qayaq escaped his powerful grip. Seeing this, the big brute roared in anger. He grabbed for Qayaq again but elusive Qayaq kept escaping his hands. In his grip, Qayaq knew he could be snapped like a dry twig. But he made up his mind he was not going to be caught. He pranced around in the middle of the *qazgi*.

The people all around were not saying anything. All were breathless, waiting in suspense. Everyone was spellbound by this extraordinary event.

Qayaq pranced around lightly, swiftly eluding the hands of the giant. The big brute was beginning to pant now, still making a rumbling noise in his throat. He tripped on one of the dead men who was flattened out on the floor. Seeing his chance, Qayaq picked him up bodily and threw him up. The leader of the trio of brutes found his big frame thrown into the air. He tried a couple of times to right himself, but he failed. He was coming down in slow motion and seeing this, Qayaq with all his might forced him to the floor. He gave him a big shove as if bouncing a ball. The big giant lay on the floor unconscious. One arm wrapped around the giant's thick neck, Qayaq squeezed hard. The big man, regaining consciousness a little, was struggling to get up. The only thing he could do was to kick the air feebly with crazy legs. The big man's thick neck was broken. His big body slackened and his broad cheeks twitched a little as he gasped his last breath.

Qayaq stood up and gazed upon the three dead men lying flat on their backs, lifeless eyes staring into nothing. "I am very sorry, but there was no way out." He addressed the people, who found their tongues and shouted at him with gratitude.

"They were nuisances to us. We were not allowed to be visited by our neighbors. Now we can bring home as many people as we want to," they shouted gratefully. In the midst of all this clamoring, Qayaq quietly dissolved into nothing. In their midst they all saw a little tiny grey fluff of down being lifted by a whiff of wind. The fluff was trembling a little and rising unsteadily. Qayaq was making his way up to the open corner of the skylight as a bit of fluff. Outside, he became a little weasel once more.

The sun was riding high when Qayaq woke up from a deep, heavy sleep. His body was numb from lying on his belly on the mountaintop all night. His eyes were full of tears as he blinked. Smarting pain made tears run down his cheeks. He felt many pin pricks all over his body as he sat up. His limbs refused to function when he tried to bend them. He knew that his soul had left his body last night, had become an animal and then became someone else to fight with the three brute leaders of the settlement. He was shaking his head to make that whining noise leave his ears. When he looked around, the earth itself was rocking. He felt very dizzy.

When he felt a little stronger, he stood up and walked around on top of the mountain. He made sure that his legs would not fold up under him before he started for the bottom of the mountain. He felt very hungry and cold, although the sun was warm and it was summer. He was chilled through and through. He was remembering now the man who's guest he had promised to be.

When he reached the village, he heard singing and laughter; it seemed to be coming from the *qazgi*. All other sod houses were quiet, so he made his way to the big structure. When he entered, young men and women were in the middle of the room dancing, the women standing on the floor not far apart from each other, the men dancers stamping their feet and waving their arms in the air, weaving among the women, who were skipping around strenuously. Singers with drums in their hands called out to them, and all at once the dancers were in a straight line facing the singers. As the singers sang a song with words, a song that told a story, dancers acted it out making motions with their arms and the movements of their bodies. In unison of movement, they looked as though one body was doing the act, their knees bending a little now and then to the beat of the drums.

Qayaq stood by the entrance watching with interest. He saw the

Drum Dancer
Eegeevudluk Ragee

man that he had met before. Absorbed in singing, eyes closed and beating on his drum, he stretched his neck, his head keeping time to the beat of the drum.

When the song was ended, the villagers all saw Qayaq standing there by the door. His host to be came forward to speak to him. He had recognized the man who had survived the rain of arrows. And turning to his people, he addressed them: "This is the man that survived many flying arrows. He shall be our first guest." Turning to Qayaq, he said, "You should have been here to see a big fight last night. Our three leaders were killed by a mighty man. You should have seen the man. He appeared out of nothing, from a fluff of down, and after he killed the three big men that ruled this community, he dissolved into nothing again. Somebody that is a powerful shaman came to set us free. In the past, the brutes had always killed our visitors. We were not allowed to be visited by outsiders.

"Now these brutes are dead and we will bring many people to our homes, many people that are like us, although the leaders did not think so. They thought we were supreme, superior to all creations. And they wanted this settlement to be protected from others.

"As soon as we dragged the bodies out, we started dancing. All night there has been rejoicing." Turning to the happy crowd again, he said, "This man shall be our first guest of honor. We shall dance and have a feast for him. And someday we will find the man who set us free and we shall make him rich!"

For an answer the crowd cheered and clapped their hands.

Qayaq was led out by his host. In his little sod house Qayaq was given some skins for bedding, skins that had been tanned nice and soft. The nice soft fur comforted Qayaq's bruised body when he went to bed.

"I'm going back to the *qazgi*," the host said. "You are tired. Sleep all day, if you want to. If you feel like eating, there is plenty of food." With these words, he left Qayaq to rejoin the dancers.

In the rosy light that came from the skylight, Qayaq inspected the interior of the soddy. The framework was of split trees that were golden brown. All were of the same material. The young trees were split and set very close together. The sod was not showing at any part of the interior. He was relieved that the people did not suspect him of killing their three former leaders. Qayaq soon fell asleep feeling warm and comforted.

When Qayaq woke up, his host was in the room moving about quietly. The fire was lit in the middle of the room and the smoke from it was making its way up to the skylight, which was uncovered. Qayaq raised his head to let his host know that he was awake. The man noticing this gave him a smile. He was very excited about what had come to pass. He said, "To think that those men that terrorized this place are now dead. Imagine that! I still cannot believe the miracle that happened last night!"

The man was looking at the one that made this incredible incident come to pass, but he did not know it. Face to face with the killer of the three tyrants, but he did not know it! Qayaq was very glad of this.

"We are going to find the mighty man who freed us and make him rich. And he shall be our Umialik." The man kept prattling on, as Qayaq gazed upon him with eyes that penetrate and could look into his soul. "If it is the last thing we do, we will find him! We will find him!" The host continued. Not knowing that Qayaq's power exceeded the powers of all their shamans' supernatural powers, he was boasting about the time that they will find the man who had saved them.

"Wherever you came from, you must not be in a rush. Why not stay and spend four days with us? We are going to have a big feast and eat, so the souls of the three men can eat and drink. We are going to dress three boys, so the souls will have clothes to wear and their immortal souls cannot come to haunt us," he said. The man was very excited. Waving his hands into the air as if to impress his listener, he kept on. "The three rascals do not deserve it, but it is our custom — whatever happens, we must carry on with our customs."*

"I am leaving tomorrow morning!" said Qayaq, who felt that he must leave.

"No, you stay with us and enjoy being the first guest of the settlement." His host was very kind but Qayaq had made up his mind to leave.

When the evening came, the men were gathering in the *qazgi*. Women and children were still at their homes. Qayaq and his host entered and sat down on the upper row of benches that was almost full already. All were quiet except for a little murmur here and there. As they sat quietly, Qayaq saw an old woman enter with a wooden platter full of food. She crossed in the middle of the room and set the platter in front of an old man, and without a word she walked out.

"Dinnertime," his host whispered to him.

Another old woman entered and found her husband and set a platter full of food in front of him and quietly walked out, neither looking right nor left. Another old woman, then another, soon every old man had a platter full of food set before him. Every woman in the same manner as the others, without lifting her eyes to meet the

*It was the Inupiat custom for the family to make a new set of clothes in honor of the deceased and to choose a special person to wear them. When my father was a young man a woman made him a complete set of clothes to wear to honor her dead son.

eyes of the man, faces straight and expressionless, looking neither right nor left. Qayaq noticed that all the women were dressed plainly but in well-made clothes.

The younger ladies were now bringing their husbands' food. With not a word or a smile, their faces a little pale and eyes downcast, they brought their husbands' food. Graceful in their movements, they looked very proud.

The girls came next one by one, never two in the *qazgi* at the same time. The girls that were too young to have husbands gave food to bachelors, widowers, and boys, probably their brothers who were old enough to be in the *qazgi* with their elders.

Toward the last, a girl dressed beautifully in spotted caribou fawn skins came in. Her clothes were trimmed with wide strips of wolverine, and everywhere that was not covered with tassels, much fancy work was showing. She made her way straight to Qayaq's host, face flushed, making her face pretty with pink cheeks between two long braids of hair that were bound with wolverine strips. She set a wooden platter full of food in front of Qayaq's host and without a word, her eyes covered with downcast black lashes, she turned around quickly. Quietly and gracefully she reached the entrance. Qayaq was very interested by this service to the men.

"My niece, my sister's daughter," the man whispered to Qayaq. "Your platter is being brought in now."

A girl a little older than the one before was walking straight toward them. Her clothes were beautifully trimmed also. She was setting a wooden platter full of food in front of Qayaq. Qayaq heard his heart pound in his ears; he feared that his host might notice. He was glad that the girl did not raise her eyes to meet his. He was sure his feelings were mirrored in his eyes. His host must have arranged this. He thought about his host and was glad that he had made up his mind that he was leaving.

"My niece, my brother's daughter," the host whispered to Qayaq about the older girl.

Qayaq felt the heat creep up to the roots of his hair. "He must have all kinds of relatives. Why wasn't I warned about this?" Qayaq felt very uncomfortable.

Qayaq, brave and never afraid to face any living thing, was for the first time afraid to meet someone's eyes, the eyes of a pretty niece of his host that he was certain could be his for the asking. But Qayaq had made up his mind that he was leaving the following morning. If he stayed — if he stayed, he knew very well he would be clay in the fair girl's pretty tapering fingers.

His embarrassment was over quickly and when he looked around the *qazgi* he was the only one that was not eating. All were not paying any attention to him, for which he was very grateful.

The wooden platter before him was new and looked as if it had never been used before. It was heaped with well-assorted food: cut up dried fish and caribou meat in one corner and a little heap of *akutuq* in another corner. In the middle were a few squares of fresh *muktuk* (black whale's skin and oil). Blended with this tasty assortment were Eskimo potatoes — very appetizing! Qayaq was tempted to eat, and he ate.

Qayaq was not yet through eating when the first old woman came in to take her platter away from her husband. All was quiet and one by one, each lady came to redeem her platter. As before, not a single woman uttering a word nor lifting her eyes to the men as she walked out gracefully and quietly. These were proud, very proud people. Dignified and well-trained, these women honored their men folks with the offering that was prepared with willing care. No wonder their leaders thought they were supreme, superior to all.

Qayaq was very glad that he had made it possible for their wish to come true — the wish to be able to have visitors from other villages. He even wondered what they would do if they all knew he himself was their savior from the terror that they had known for many years. How many young men were killed in front of their unblinking eyes, how many young men had begged for mercy? Mercy that was never granted. Think of all the many years in which unaware young men had stumbled into the village, never to escape alive, never to return to their parents.

Then one year an unaware young man, Qayaq, had stumbled into the village while he was seeking to return to his parents, who maybe even now were looking forward to his arrival.

Now the people were very happy about not having to see any more killings. For four days they were going to celebrate the deaths of their three former leaders, after which their shamans were going to perform and try to find out who was the person that had set them free. "Somebody at some other village must have found out about our cruel leaders and through supernatural power came to destroy the ones that made many people suffer," an elder said.

The men were singing and the few elderly men were beating on their drums when the women began to file into the *qazgi*. Someone stood up and was dancing alone, and another joined him. Soon the big *qazgi* was throbbing with singing, shouting and stamping of the feet, amid peals of laughter from the girls that were not dancing. When the dancing was in full swing, the big structure was shaking with the vibration of the dancers on the floor.

Qayaq's host was among them, weaving his way among women dancers and, with body rigid, waving his arms. Lifting his feet off the floor, he sang, "Ooi-ooi-ooi-ooi," making his whole body shake, bending his knees now and then, making himself look short and then tall again. "Ooi-ooi, whoo-whoo-whook!" He was very much absorbed in dancing strenuously.

The next morning, when Qayaq insisted on leaving, the people made him take a *kayagiaq* (kayak that seats two persons with no top) for a gift. He was very happy to accept the wonderful gift. The people felt that they must give him something because he was their first guest.

The *kayagiaq*, the frame of which was thin birch and bound together with *ugruk* (bearded seal) rope, was covered with *ugruk* skin. The hair was removed from the sealskin, and the tough golden brown leather was almost transparent. As Qayaq paddled, the *kayagiaq* skimmed over the water lightly.

Qayaq paddled and paddled.

He was going down the Noatak River, paddling with the current this time. The villagers advised against paddling with the current, but Qayaq was very brave and did not care what should happen to him. The east wind was blowing softly and the summer was almost over and soon it would be fall. The sun was warm on his left as he faced the west to follow the large river that must lead to his wife, Umialik's daughter. He had promised to go back to her someday, and someday he was going home to see his parents.

He did not have to travel far when he came around a large bend. He saw in the near distance two big jagged rocks that were the banks of the river. They were banging together. Fitting tight together, they met, like teeth that were ready to chew, with a loud bang that split the quietness. He saw and knew the two rocks had killed many. No wonder the villagers tried to stop him from following the current. He was not paddling now but his birch *kayagiaq* was speeding toward the banging rocks. They would separate and bang together again.

Qayaq looked around him. He saw nothing but water all around him that seemed to be standing still now, compared to the speed

of the *kayagiaq* that was uncontrollably speeding straight for
the banging rocks that were the banks of the river.
Somehow he must slow down the little *kayagiaq* that he was
sure was not responsible for what was happening. The craft
was speeding like it was being towed by something unseen,
heading on straight for the banging, jagged rocks. It was
going so fast that in his ears he heard a whirring noise, noise
that blended with the song that his father sang for him when
he was leaving: "May the desire to save the human race be
your strength and your guide."

His father's words Qayaq was remembering now. He
must — he must somehow survive this evil trap! His birch
kayagiaq was not going very fast now, but the two jagged
rocks that are on each side of the river were slowly coming
to meet each other. As if they knew that Qayaq was very
near — too terribly close! Somehow his father's song with
supernatural power was delaying the speeding *kayagiaq*.

Then when he was a few yards away from the living
rocks, he desperately thought of the three magic pebbles
that his father had made him swallow. Making a gurgling sound in
his throat, he forced one of them up into his mouth. It was alive, it
was pulsating! He dared not keep it in his mouth. The jagged
rocks were about to bang together, terrifyingly close. Just as he
thought for a moment he would be crushed by them, with all his
might he spit the little pebble out of his mouth and saw it land
between the two rocks that bang together hard. There was a loud
crash. The two rocks smashed together, into bits like pebbles, and
were sinking harmlessly to the depths of the deep wide river.
Qayaq, with his hands on each side of the *kayagiaq,* sailed over the
swirling, rumbling water and when he reached safety, he looked
back and he saw nothing but a whirlpool that the many pebbles of

Kuuqapik (The River)
Pitseolak Niviaqsi

sinking rock had left.

The *kayagiaq* was not speeding now, just easily riding the current of the Noatak River. Now that the banging rocks were gone, the Noatak River was open to be travelled forever. The little pebble that his father had made him swallow accompanied by a magic word had saved him. Somewhere — somewhere in his body was another one like it. What he would use it against, he did not know. He was led by an unseen hand and many exciting events awaited him in all corners of the Eskimo world, but what they could be, of course, he was not aware of.

On the bank of the river, he saw an old man. He was sitting on the ground. How long had he been sitting here? He was very grey and wrinkled. When he noticed Qayaq he called to him. "Is there enough room for two in your *kayagiaq*? I want a ride, Qayaq; I am your uncle." The old man was calling him by his name. How did he know his name? Qayaq pretended he was not interested. But he beached his *kayagiaq* and let the old man come aboard.

For many days they travelled, going around the bends in the river, the old man always sitting in the *kayagiaq* in the same position. When Qayaq left the *kayagiaq* and looked around the riverbank, the old man never said a word, always sitting quietly with his head hanging down in front of him. He never asked where and why Qayaq was going. He always seemed to be half-dozing in the *kayagiaq*.

One bright afternoon Qayaq noticed a portage on the right side of the river. Straight, short willows bordered it. When he beached the *kayagiaq*, he looked into the water on his left. There in the water was a woman. She was looking up at him smiling. Why was she in the water? Suddenly Qayaq felt that he had to get her out of the water. She might drown in there, even though she was looking like it was natural for her to be where she was. But Qayaq was eager to right the wrong and dove into the water after her. Inside the water, he could not find her. Kicking with his legs and making powerful strokes with his arms, he investigated but he could not find her. Coming up close to his *kayagiaq,* he came aboard and looked into the water again, and there in the water was that same pretty woman looking up at him smiling. Qayaq, diving after her, repeated his effort to save her, but like before came up with clothes dripping wet, clinging tightly to his body. Why was he seeing the image of the pretty woman in the water? Qayaq could not understand. His uncle as usual was not paying any attention to him. He thought to ask him but decided not to bother him. Maybe he would think he was crazy anyway — seeing a pretty woman in the water.

Looking like a drowned caribou, he left his uncle behind and following the portage he investigated. There at the other end of it was a large sod house. Smoke was curling out of the skylight. On reaching it, he entered. There by the fire sat the woman that was smiling up at him out of the water. Young and pretty, she was looking up and smiling with that same smile on her face.

"I am to have very pleasant company! Give me some dry clothes — it is your fault I am wet clear through! Imagine leaving your image in the water!" Qayaq pretended to be very mad at the pretty woman. Without saying a word, the same whimsical smile on her face, she was reaching for a set of clothes that was hanging on the wall. Qayaq saw many other sets of clothes that appeared to belong to men. Some clothing was very large, and some looked as if it belonged to small men.

"Do you live alone?" he asked the woman that was chattering now. Qayaq's asking for a change of clothes seemed to please her very much.

"My mother and father are out. They do the hunting and I keep the fire going," she answered. "They ought to be home soon."

The interior of the room was black and shiny with old smoke. Looking around Qayaq could not make out the framework of the structure. The young woman set out a wooden platter full of food. She was talking now very good naturedly. She was laughing aloud, too. She was so friendly that Qayaq was very suspicious. Once in a while he heard a swishing sound from somewhere. Funny, there was no breeze outside. He looked around. He did not notice anything out of the ordinary. Seeing this, the girl was laughing, as loud as she could.

"Come, come, let me in on the joke. I won't mind laughing with you," Qayaq said to her. But the young woman kept right on laughing, with pretty rippling and vibrant laughter. Somewhere from the house Qayaq was hearing that swishing sound. It was quiet awhile. Now Qayaq concentrated on the swishing sound alone. The girl was trying to distract his attention from it with her laughter. There it came again. This time a little louder — that certain swishing something seemed to be coming closer and closer.

While eating, he stayed on the alert. He knew there was something wrong in this sod house that was black and shiny inside, with a laughing young woman as an occupant. But what, he could not make out. Was he in an evil death trap? There it comes again, and looking backwards quickly, he saw part of the wall moving as if to take its natural place. There, he had it in his mind that the wall was stretching like rubber and was trying to touch his back! He pretended that he did not notice, chewed on the food that was set in front of him, while the interior of the house was roaring now with the ringing of the woman's laughter. There again came that swishing sound. He looked at the wall that was stretching out to touch him. Qayaq moved away a little for it was very close this time. Reaching out for it, he touched the black shiny surface with his fingertips and it was sticky.

"So, that is your game, how many have you killed in this manner!" He shouted at the woman, but the woman was too busy laughing to do any answering. He filled the wooden platter with the ashes from the fire, which was smoldering now, and threw the ashes at the wall, and all the specks of grey ashes spread over the sticky wall. All over the surface of the black shiny interior, there was nothing but gritty grey powdery ashes. The young woman was not laughing now. She had been killing many people, making them stick to the wall, and a man stuck to the wall was helpless. Many men were killed by this pretty laughing woman.

Having destroyed one more evil death trap, Qayaq made his way to his *kayagiaq*. His uncle was still sitting as usual in it. He launched it and continued the journey over the Noatak River, with water that flowed peacefully and quietly, with young willows and trees mirrored in its glassy edges.

Finally and at last his uncle raised his head and looked back at Qayaq. His face was grey and wrinkled, his hair almost white from age. "Thank you very much for the ride, it is about time I travel by myself. You are a patient young man. Whatever happens, may luck always be with you. You have been very kind to me." Qayaq let him out of his *kayagiaq* on the right side of the river and watched him take off. On four legs the old man was running. Qayaq saw a lynx running away from him. An animal! "Why do animals and birds appear to me as humans?" Qayaq asked himself. The old man that claimed to be his uncle was an animal, a lynx.* No wonder he was always waiting for him in his *kayagiaq*. Always patiently waiting for his return, no matter how long he was away from the *kayagiaq*.

Qayaq paddled and paddled.

Not long after he came upon cannibals, a very large village

*This is Qayaq's uncle who went north when Qayaq's parents settled at the mouth of the Selawik River after their parents were killed. This is reported at the beginning of the epic. Qayaq's uncle was looking in the south for his son, Ukuunaaqtuaq who had actually gone north. Like Qayaq and his eleven brothers, Ukuunaaqtuaq had never returned home. Daniel Foster told me about Ukuunaaqtuaq in 1975. His stories of Qayaq and Ukuunaaqtuaq will be the subject of a future book.

inhabited by many people that live on human meat. For many days, he was among them. Wherever he went, he was followed. He took advantage of this and lectured to them about people that are living today — like them. The people they killed wanted to live — so, "Why not live on animal and other game? There are many other things to eat on this earth besides human beings. After all, the strangers that you kill to eat were born to people that are probably now looking for their return. Can't you see the suffering you have caused many a parent? How would you like it if one of your sons never came back from a hunting trip?"

Qayaq was shouting at them. "I'm sure you would not like that — that would just about kill some of you with grief!"

Qayaq was still with these cannibals when the word reached him that his brother wanted Qayaq to come and help him. Someone told Qayaq that his brother was defending a big village up at Utqiugvik (Point Barrow) from a big sea-going mole that was trying to kill the people. And the big mole was beginning to overpower Qayaq's brother.

At last, at long last! He was hearing something about one of his brothers. He was overjoyed by this. Someday — someday he was going home to his parents. And he would have news about one brother. But where were the other ten? He knew he was the twelfth son. And how did his brother know where he was? How did he know that he existed?

For many days Qayaq travelled north and when he reached a large village, the brother, who was older, was doing his best to defend many people. The big water mole was coming up out of the ocean and there Qayaq's brother made an effort to kill him, hitting him many times everywhere on his body while dodging away from his appetite, but the big mole was too large an animal to kill. There on the shore in front of many igloos was his brother and in the water a mountain of a mole was trying to land so he could take one of the younger men to eat, always picking on the best and youngest.

"The mole has taken a few already. No matter what I did, he was too much for me, so I sent for you," the brother said. "He lives in the water and these last few days he has been persistent."

Qayaq dove into the water without a word, a knife in hand. He swam after the large mole. He was completely out of sight and the big mole swimming with eyes above the water could not see him. Somehow, somehow Qayaq had to mount him before the enormous mole reached the shoreline. He was close to it now. Somehow he found himself riding the swimming mole. At this, he was so surprised, he rode the startled mole a few yards. Who threw him on the enraged monster? Who was always granting his wishes? He knew he was not responsible for mounting, but this he could not solve in his mind. Or had the magic power of the *akutuq* that he had taken a taste of helped him again?

There he was, entwined around the neck of the enraged mole. It was so large that his legs and arms were only half way around the neck, the neck of the growling, barking, and enraged mole. It was rolling around, trying to free itself from the iron-like grip of Qayaq. Qayaq knew he could not kill the animal by choking it. So he was using his knife, but the knife for the first time was too short. The stone knife was too small a weapon for such an enormous animal. It was the only weapon he had with him, so somehow he had to use it against the growling, barking, and rolling animal. In this terrible watery struggle he knew he had no choice of weapons. So with his knife, he hacked at the neck of the mole. The fur was so shaggy and coarse that at first he thought he would never touch the vital parts of the mole, but having something to do drove him on.

Qayaq raised his head when he was out of the water for just an instant and saw his brother running back and forth on the shore.

He was going to help when and if the animal decided to go ashore. Qayaq felt the only thing to do now was to make his knife strike at one spot, the spot where the collarbone should be. With eyes closed and teeth set tight, and legs and one arm hanging on tightly, Qayaq was striking with his knife with all the strength he could gather from his powerful body. The angry mole was rolling in the water very swiftly now.

Qayaq knew that it was feeling the sting from the wound that his knife was making. Feeling himself about to come up to the surface, he opened his eyes and in that split second he saw the water growing pink with blood. In a flash he was under the water again, and up to the surface again for a breath, then under again. Feeling the pain in his neck, the mole was rolling around very, very fast in an effort to throw Qayaq off his shoulders. Each time Qayaq looked in the direction of the shoreline, they were coming closer to it.

Finally and at last, the big monster was slowing down his rolling in the water. Qayaq knew the ferocious mole was growing weak. The struggle was long and violent. Qayaq was very tired, too, and was glad that the big mole had decided to edge toward the shoreline. The big mole was not rolling now and did not seem to care about Qayaq riding on his shoulders. He must know that the shoreline was close. He swam easily for it, and looking back Qayaq saw that they made a red streak on the open sea. He was very grateful for this for he was suddenly very tired.

On reaching the shore, Qayaq jumped off his mount and said to his brother. "He's yours now, I want you to give the final blow!" His brother stuck his long knife into the chest of the dying animal.

This prehistoric creature had eaten men from the village. The villagers had been forced to stay home from hunting. Some of the bravest had come out of their huts to help Qayaq's brother, only to be devoured by the hungry mole.

Qayaq's brother was very strong and quick in movement, and he had been the only one who could ward off this man-eater. All these years he had righted the wrong and defended the weak all along the northwestern coast of Alaska. Like Qayaq he had destroyed many evil traps that killed men. Where were the other ten brothers? Have they gone to all parts of the world to save the human race? Or did they all get killed like many, many men? They did not know. But someday they were going back home to see their parents. This they vowed to each other — to the parents that had waited for their twelve sons who never came back.

Somewhere close to Qikiqtaqruk (which means "big island," Herschel Island), spring was in the air when Qayaq stood on top of a good-sized mountain, watching a large village below — a village with a shaman for a leader. The *Angatkuq* (shaman) was always sitting on top of a large hut, always on the look-out. He was sitting at his lookout place this early morning. Sitting erect, straining his eyes into the distance, never missing anything to see or to hear. Qayaq saw him and gazed upon him with eyes that penetrate and could see into one's soul.

Angatkuq was not mean to him, but Qayaq saw what was in his heart. From morning till night, the man had always been on the look-out. By this large structure there was another one like it. And Qayaq saw that this shaman lived in one of them and his children occupied the other. Qayaq heard him calling to his daughter, "Get the place ready; somebody is on the mountain!" Qayaq was very surprised about this; he knew that he could not be seen with ordinary eyes.

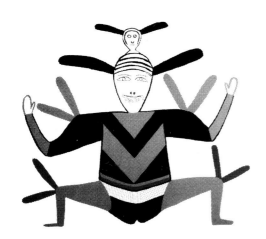

Angutkoq
Jessie Oonark

The daughter had always waited on her father and had always obeyed and trusted him. But there was one thing she would not grant him — taking a husband that would be his choice. This *Nii-viq-siq* (young lady) had been single for many years, although her older brother and her younger brother had taken wives. Many suitors Nii-viq-siq had had, but she had made up her mind that she was going to stay single. No matter what they did to her she could not be taken for a wife.

This village was never freely visited by outsiders. Anyone who dared to enter the village was killed by the shaman and his two sons. When the man was too strong to be killed, he was not allowed to leave. Once entering, he was made to die or to stay. Those allowed to live helped support the whole community.

On top of the mountain, Qayaq understood all this as he gazed upon it with eyes that penetrate and can look into one's soul. He knew that he could not reach the village without being seen. Angatkuq was more alert now. He was excited about a possible victim that was close at hand. The only time he was happy was when competing with a stranger that happened to stumble into their village, unsuspicious of evil rites. To bolster his powers, Qayaq took a taste of the *akutuq* given him by his mother.

Before he knew what was happening, he found himself being a little weasel. He changed into this shape bodily this time. He came down the mountain as a weasel toward the Angatkuq, weaving through large tussocks and grass. Weaving toward the village, he noticed that the terrain was becoming rougher. He had come down nearly to the village, but Angatkuq was not aware of him. So very absorbed in his trying to see a man, he did not see a little brown weasel flashing among the large tussocks and grass. Finally there was nothing to hide him. He was running on bare gravel. Qayaq was sure he could be detected running on bare gravel.

Angatkuq was looking all around him fast. He knew there was somebody very close. He felt that somebody was very close, but he could not see him. He was now frantic with fear. Somebody for the first time was almost upon him. He knew this, but he could not see him. On reaching the edge of the grass, Qayaq changed into a little fluff of down, and the wind favored him. He was sailing over the pebbles, and Angatkuq was very close now. He was standing on top of his large igloo and was looking far away. An ugly scowl on his face, he fumed and grunted like he would like to have a fight with somebody. There was some powerful soul near at hand; still he could not see him. This made him very furious at himself. Able to see anything supernatural, still he could not see Qayaq, although sensing that he was very near.

Qayaq, as a little fluff of down, made his way to the door of the big ugly man's house and when he reached it he became himself again and said, "So you think you are the most powerful Angatkuq on earth! We shall see who is stronger in strength or in supernatural powers. I was in plain view and you could not see me! I could have killed you if I wanted to, but I am always fair to my opponents."

This made Angatkuq furious. Seeing somebody for the first time reach the village without being seen was unbearable to him. To be able to protect his large village was his pride.

Qayaq said, "I am here to be your opponent." Qayaq's great heart was pounding from excitement.

When Angatkuq recovered from surprise, he leaped from the top of the domelike sod hut, but Qayaq was too quick for him. He was inside the large house already. This sod hut was very large. Inside there was a little platform built all around against the wall. Above

Untitled [Weasel]
Kanayuk Tukalak

it was another platform wide enough for a person to sit on. Three rows of people were able to look on whatever was happening in the big structure. These *ik-liqs* (platforms) were full of spectators already. Knowing that a stranger was near, Angatkuq had made them assemble in his house while he was still on the look-out.

In the middle of the room was a long sharp rock, ugly and protruding from the floor. On it was a large stain of dark blood. Qayaq knew that it was human blood, probably some innocent victim that did not know the history of this village.

As soon as Angatkuq raged into the room, he grabbed Qayaq on the shoulders. "You impudent young fool, maybe you can sneak in, but you are not going to leave this place! You will get killed or you stay! Most of the young fools like you meet death in this house!"

All was quiet, everyone holding his breath, everyone watching two big powerful men gripping each other on their shoulders. Sizing up each other's strength, they stood leaning on to each other beside the gruesome sharp rock. Finally Angatkuq lifted Qayaq into the air and was going to slam him down on the knife-like rock. Qayaq yanked himself loose from Angatkuq's grip and sailed over the hideous rock. Landing easily on his feet, he heard the many gasps and murmurs of the crowd, and this made Angatkuq more furious. They gripped each other again and like before Angatkuq lifted Qayaq into the air and this time he was not letting Qayaq slip out of his grip as he tried to slam him down on the rock, but he saw Qayaq set himself free and sail clean over the protruding rock and land on the other side. They fought all day.

Never once did Qayaq try to slam Angatkuq on the rock. He only defended himself from getting killed.

When night came, Angatkuq was tired and told Qayaq so. "Let us rest now. Tomorrow I will try and kill you." Angatkuq was not mad now. He told Qayaq that he was wonderful in sailing over the rock. He told him that others had never done that.

The room was filled with compliments for Qayaq. Everyone was happy to see the match. Everyone seemed to be glad that he escaped death.

From the lowest rows of people a little boy stood up and approached Qayaq. He was shabbily dressed, his rosy-cheeked face lit up with smiles. "I want you to be my guest. My grandmother and I live at the end of the village. Many times I have wished to have the strangers for our guests, but I could never express my feelings until now. Seeing you, I did not feel bashful anymore." Speaking thus, the little orphan was excited. Qayaq was touched by the sincerity of the little boy, and thought how cute he was.

"I will be very glad to be your guest. I am very glad you asked me," was all Qayaq could say to the pretty boy. The hint of tears trembled with his last words. Unexpected kindness from a mere child was something enormous to this greatest man of great men. The man that could turn into anything at his own will and could dissolve into thin air was led on by an unseen hand to destroy evil death traps and right wrong.

He was led out of Angatkuq's gruesome dwelling by the little boy he had made happy by accepting his invitation. They passed many dwellings, some large and some small. At the end of the row, they entered a little igloo, the interior almost bare. The grandmother was a very old woman, sitting by the flames of the fire in the middle of the room.

"I am very glad my grandson had the nerve to ask you to be our guest. You are very welcome here, but you can see that we are very poor. However, we will do the best we can for you," she said.

Qayaq knew the sincerity of the old lady's words and did not wish to have any better hostess.

"Angatkuq has killed many people," the grandmother continued. "I have wished to help many a young man. But I could not volunteer my ability to help. I will try and help you to the best of what I am able to do." This old woman was not talking like she was an ordinary human being!

Qayaq spent the night with the grandson and the grandmother at the end of a long line of homes. Early in the morning someone called down from the skylight — "Angatkuq is ready for Qayaq." That was all he said.

From her little sewing basket Qayaq's hostess dug up a little tiny sewing bead and told Qayaq to swallow it. Qayaq swallowed it. "If you have anything with you, now is the time to call on your helper," she told him.

"I have no one to call on," said Qayaq, pulling some *akutuq* from under his arm. "This is what my mother made for me when I was leaving home. I am my parents' twelfth son. Eleven left as I did and never came back. I found one but I do not know what happened to the other ten."

Qayaq for the first time felt free to talk about his brothers and his parents. "I am going home someday — I promised myself this — this pebble that my father gave me is going back to them someday." Remembering what had happened he had a faraway look in his eyes, as he reverently remembered his mother saying, "The blood I shed into this *akutuq* shall be your youth and your strength." He now took a taste.

In Angatkuq's house again he was face-to-face with a strong brute that had snuffed life out of so many men with the help of the sharp, protruding, gruesome rock set in the middle of the floor. The people had already assembled in the round shape of Angatkuq's dwelling.

Somewhere, somewhere among them was a shabbily dressed little boy pulling for him. The little boy had a cute face with rosy cheeks and brown eyes. He showed in his eyes hero worship for Qayaq, as he might for a wonderful older brother.

Like the day before, the shaman was going to fight Qayaq, trying to throw him and slam him down on the bloodthirsty sharp rock. Like the day before, Qayaq kept freeing himself from the savage grip of Angatkuq and, each time, sailed over the rock out of danger.

Without stopping for rest and food, Angatkuq tried to kill Qayaq, but Qayaq never once made an effort to kill his opponent, just protected himself from getting killed. Finally Angatkuq was tired, and he called for his older son. The son was large and strong like his father. Using his father's methods, he worked on Qayaq but he could not slam Qayaq on the rock. When his older son became tired, Angatkuq called on his younger son who was, like his father, large and strong.

The second son did his best to kill Qayaq, but Qayaq was too quick in movement and always set himself free in the air, no matter how savage the grip of the other was. Finally and at last the night came. Angatkuq and his sons were too tired to do anything else, but Qayaq asked if there was anybody else in the room who would like to try to slam him on the rock. But no one said a word.

The little boy came forward to take Qayaq home. The grandmother said with enthusiasm, "You were wonderful! I was very glad that you never tried to kill the brute!"

"Grandma, I did not see you there! How did you know?" the little boy asked.

"Of course, you couldn't see me! Silly! You think I'll come and let everyone know that I'd cheapen myself being seen there?" she retorted at her grandson. "I was by the entrance of the evil house though." She had come invisibly, ashamed to let anyone know she was interested in Angatkuq's killings, still too curious to stay away from Qayaq's fight. She was a very proud woman, far from ordinary in having supernatural powers. What had cast this high-born woman down to bare necessities? That proud appearance still lived on in her proud soul — never as long as she lived would she be abased in her spirit. She patted Qayaq on his back, and to his surprise a little bead came up to his mouth. He spit it out on his hand, and the bead looked same as it was before he swallowed it. The grand-mother took it and shoved the little bead back into her sewing basket.

That night Qayaq could not sleep. Although the grandmother told him not to be on the alert, he could not sleep.

The third and the last day of fighting dawned too soon. It was bright and very early when Angatkuq's messenger came.

"Angatkuq is ready for Qayaq."

From the smoke hole of the humble dwelling came the message as before.

Like the morning before, Qayaq was made to swallow the little bead, after which he took a taste of the *akutuq* his mother had given him.

When he entered Angatkuq's dwelling, the house was already full of spectators. At the rear the two sons sat, with bows and arrows poised to strike at Qayaq.

Angatkuq was sitting close to his sons. This time Qayaq was going to be tried with arrows. One of them sent an arrow with a terrific force behind it. As the arrow sped at him, Qayaq side-stepped and caught it in his hand by the stem. There were many gasps of breath from the audience. Another came, and another. Each one Qayaq did not fail to catch by the stem. And every arrow he caught was broken in two by one powerful hand. All that morning many arrows sped to him, only to be caught and broken.

Angatkuq finally made his two sons quit. "You'll never get him. This ends our fight with Qayaq," he addressed the cheering crowd. "You are now one of us, you will not be permitted to leave the village," he said to Qayaq. "You will hunt and help support my people. If you know what is good for you, you will not try and sneak away."

"If I am to stay here all my life, why not give me your daughter for my wife?" Qayaq challenged him. Angatkuq was quiet.

Nii-viq-siq (young lady) could wrap Angatkuq around her little finger. She had refused to accept a husband so far.

"If you can win her, you can have her, but of this I cannot promise you," the Angatkuq finally said.

And, as before, Nii-viq-siq refused to become a wife. "Doesn't everybody know that I shall never accept a man for a husband? I should think this is understood by now." Qayaq was informed of her bold words. Angatkuq was for the first time furious at his daughter and threatened to harm her. Hearing about this Qayaq entered Angatkuq's dwelling and told him to hold his wrath at least for a few days.

"Leave it to me, maybe I could do something without your help," Qayaq said to Angatkuq.

Qayaq was going to do his best to win the girl who had refused so many suitors. He went in and out of the big house that was occupied by Nii-viq-siq, her two brothers and their two wives. He visited them and spent many hours with them. The brothers and their wives liked him very much, but they could not do anything to make Nii-viq-siq change her mind.

Nii-viq-siq sat many hours sewing quietly in her own corner of the house, never once meeting Qayaq's eyes, never once taking part in the conversations or sharing food.

When she became hungry, she left the house and went to her

father's house to eat. On these occasions, her father begged her to take Qayaq for her husband. "You will never run across a greater man than Qayaq. I beg of you this. Don't you see I am growing old and will not be able to support you soon?" Nii-viq-siq never said a word. When she had finished eating, she would walk out of her father's house and enter her own to sit down in her own corner and sew, never lifting her face to look at Qayaq. Qayaq was patient but soon he gave up. Seeing this, Angatkuq was very angry and told everybody to gather at his place.

"We are going to leave Nii-viq-siq, my stubborn daughter, alone in this village. We will take everything away with us, so she will not have anything to live on. She has refused the man I want for a son-in-law; she shall pay for this by dying alone in the deserted village! Everyone must see that he does not forget anything." Everyone filed out without a word. Everyone must obey Angatkuq's orders.

All the skin boats were to be filled with their belongings, and each and every house must be left bare. The big village was going to be deserted with Angatkuq's daughter as its only occupant.

"If you are able to escape, you must get away at the last minute," the old woman told Qayaq. "I think Angatkuq means to go very far."

The younger sister-in-law of Nii-viq-siq was very pretty, kind hearted, and loved Nii-viq-siq very much. She told her husband, Angatkuq's younger son, that she meant to do something about the situation. But her husband, fearing his father, told her to forget it, if she had a wild idea.

"All right, if you will not help me smuggle your sister in our boat, you can at least help me leave some food anyway. It's a shame to be throwing away a lovely person like her. And to think it is over not wanting a husband." The young sister-in-law pouted all day and refused to be kind to her husband until he promised to help her out.

They filled a seal-poke full of dried meat, *muktuk* and some oil.

They planned to hide this in one of the igloos, along with some clothes and two *ulus* (women's knives). The sister-in-law secretly told Nii-viq-siq about this. She was left by the others with not a single thing, just the clothes she wore.

Many departing skin boats Nii-viq-siq watched from the top of her igloo, skin boats laden with her people and their belongings. Her parents, brothers, and her sisters-in-law rowed away from the village, never to see her again. She was far from happy as she gazed upon them until she could not see them anymore. She was left to starve to death alone in this deserted village — just because — just because she did not want a husband. If she had to do it all over again, she would not have done otherwise.

For many days she lived on the food that was left by her sister-in-law. Many early mornings found her sitting on top of her large igloo, looking in the direction that her people took. She hoped that her father might change his mind and send her brothers after her. Day after day waiting and waiting for her brothers who did not come. Although she ate sparingly, her store of food was growing smaller and smaller. Finally there was enough left for only a few more meals. If she wanted to live, she knew she must do something. Her folk had left her to die, so she might as well not grieve over them.

When she sat on her house and was on the lookout, she noticed a large wolf coming close to the village, and seeing her he would run away. Now and then that large wolf came near, only to run away again.

One early morning, she made ready to leave. She put new clothes on and taking the little food that was left and the two *ulus*, started off facing inland. In the distance she saw that same large wolf.

On reaching the mountains, she climbed one of them and followed a little creek downward and reached the bottom. When she reached

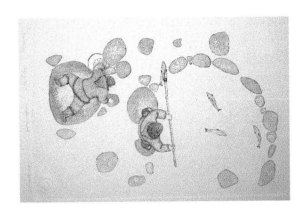

Char Fishing
Andrew Karpik

a broad stream, she noticed that there were some fish in it. She decided that she must try to catch them; so she built a weir out of young trees and willows with the help of her larger *ulu.*

All that summer she caught and worked on fish. She dried many and built a cache to store them in. When she was sure she would be well off here, she built a little igloo. Many times she saw a wolf; from afar the wolf watched her when she worked. The wolf came nearer and nearer each time he showed himself. All summer long Nii-viq-siq worked and lived on fish. The fall would soon come around. She must put up enough to last her the whole winter.

One early morning, she was sitting under her fish racks again when a young stranger came, very good-natured, tall and very good looking. His clothes were made of *sik-sik* (ground squirrel) trimmed with wolf and wolverine. Nii-viq-siq was very happy to see the man. She must not be so far from some people. The young man looked tired and had nothing with him but the knife that was hanging from his belt.

"I am very hungry. Have you anything to eat?" he asked.

"I have plenty to eat but everything is fish. I have some dried fish, cooked fish and fish oil. I cannot catch anything but fish." Nii-viq-siq felt very humble about the kind of food she had to live on.

"That would be the kind of food I would like to eat most." The young man was going to be pleasant and easy to feed. Never before had she served willingly. For the first time, she wanted to please a young man. She ate and enjoyed eating for the first time, and the young man ate with relish. The dried fish, he said, he had not tasted for a long, long time. Nii-viq-siq enjoyed his company so much that she hated to see him leave. After he ate, they sat around the bonfire

LELA KIANA OMAN

and talked awhile. Nii-viq-siq was eager to hear about where he came from and how far the place he came from was, but she did not dare be so forward as to ask him. When the afternoon came, he left her without saying anything about his home.

Next day, she saw a wolf not very far from her igloo. Funny she did not mention it to the man. He had asked if he could come to see her again, and she had told him that he could come anytime. She was very glad he wanted to come again. So from day to day she had something to look forward to. But the young man did not come for four days. Why? Did she appear too eager for him to come again? She almost wished that she had refused him when he asked if he could come again. She was worried and upset for fear that he would not come again. The showing up of that wolf did not help any. He appeared to become more and more tame, and she did not have anything to kill him with. Funny that when the evening came, he always left. If he should attack her, she thought of her big *ulu* as a possible weapon.

On the fifth day, the young man came, looking handsome, and he looked very happy. This time without asking him, she set some food for him and ate with him. She was so happy about his coming, she did not care at the time what he would think about her. He stayed and talked to her. When the afternoon came, he made ready to depart.

"You have been very kind to me. I wonder if there is anything you would like best to eat, that I might be able to bring you," he said.

"Oh, bring me some dried caribou meat! I hope this isn't too much to ask for," she said excitedly. She was so very eager — thinking of the food that she used to eat at her father's house, that she forgot to control herself.

The Shaman Becomes a Wolf
Myra Kukiiyaut

"Don't worry, I will bring you some. We have plenty of it at home," he answered.

Nii-viq-siq climbed on her igloo to watch him leave. He stopped a couple of times to look back.

This kind man in the *sik-sik* (squirrel) parka kept coming to visit her, bringing her things that she would like to eat. The wolf that she kept seeing protected her. That was Qayaq in the form of a wolf as well as the man in the *sik-sik* parka. And not too long after he took her where people lived — many people.

But the story does not say that Qayaq married her and made her his wife. This could also be understood since in the beginning she did not want to become a wife. He respected that.

This ends the reading of the writing I did in 1947. These stories I heard as I was growing up with my father, Jim Kiana and my aunt, Susie Lockhart, both of the Kobuk Valley. Additions to the old stories and some new stories were told to me by several Inupiat who came to the road house in Candle. They were Frieda and Charlie Goodwin of Selawik, George and Flora Washington, and Jim Hadley, all of Buckland. There are some more stories that I heard over the years that I would like to add to the Epic of Qayaq. *I will try and go on with them.*

L E L A   K I A N A   O M A N

After Qayaq travelled on Noatak River he was known to have paddled down the Yukon River.

He paddled and paddled.

While he was paddling down, he saw a portage that was cut through many willows. At the end of the portage that was on the bank of the river, he saw something that was shiny and beautiful. It jutted out of the ground looking like a monument. It was so beautiful that he could not resist going closer to see what it was. Even though he knew there were dangers, he had to see it.

When he came up to it, he touched it, and his hand stuck. He tried to pull away from it and his other hand was stuck, too. He used his feet to try to get himself free and his feet were also stuck. He knew that this was a trap and he was caught. He heard someone coming from the land side. When the person came close, he noticed that he had a mouth reaching up to his ears. He was a human being but he had a huge mouth that reached up to his ears. When he saw that the strange man's trap had caught him, Qayaq pretended to be dead. The man set him free, tied him up and picked him up on his back to carry him home.

On the way Qayaq could feel willows rubbing against him. He caught one of them in his hand and the man thought that he was caught in snags and said, "A, a, a, *naktaqasri, naktaqasri*," which means, "a, a, a, let's not get stuck. Let's not get stuck." This amused Qayaq so much that he kept doing it. When they passed the portage, he saw a huge dwelling. Outside of the house was a cache on stilts. A little boy came out of the house and was very excited. He said, "My father got me human eyes to eat." Knowing that the boy was very excited, Qayaq dared to open his eyes. He looked at the little boy and noticed that he had a mouth that reached up to his ears like his father. This made him look very hideous.

The 'Evil Spirit' Expects
to Devour the Man
Lukassie Tukalak

Qayaq was taken inside the family's large dwelling and was put on a shelf to thaw out. He pretended to be frozen by keeping his muscles very taut. The mother of the family felt him and knew that he was frozen solid. She had taken her huge *ulu* out to butcher Qayaq. She knew that this catch was too frozen so she left him lying on the shelf. The mother also had a mouth that reached up to her ears like the rest of her family. Soon after, the family made ready to go to sleep.

Before they lay down, the little boy was playing on the floor. When he came near, Qayaq opened one eye and looked at him. The boy said excitedly, "The eye that I am going to eat opened up and looked at me!"

His parents did not pay any attention to him. Qayaq knew they thought that he was just playing. After a bit, Qayaq knew that the boy was staring at his face again and he opened both eyes. The little boy said, "Both eyes that I am going to eat looked at me!"

The parents did not pay any attention to the boy.

The boy said, "That man is alive!"

The parents heeded him not.

The family lay down, and soon all were asleep. There was a stone under Qayaq's head. He picked this up and let it drop on top of the father's head and killed him. He picked a second stone up and let it drop on the mother's head and killed her. There was still this little boy sleeping. Qayaq felt very sorry for him; the boy looked helpless and innocent, but Qayaq knew that people who have mouths reaching up to their ears are dangerous and must not survive.

He did not stay there long. He left after killing this family.

Qayak paddled and paddled.

He travelled down the Yukon River. At the mouth of this river he came upon a large village. Same as before, as in other villages, there was an Umialik, a man that ruled over the whole village. These people lived off both sea and land animals. Qayaq was told that there was one creature that nobody could kill. It was a bird, a ptarmigan. This ptarmigan was this Umialik's pet. It was so huge and fierce that every time it exhaled there was fire shooting out of its mouth. This fire coming out of its mouth killed people.

Not long after he reached the settlement, Qayaq became the Umialik's son-in-law. As time went on, children were born to Qayaq and his wife. During all this time Umialik was trying to kill his son-in-law, but did not succeed. One day the Umialik said that he would like to have the ptarmigan killed and used for the feast that the village was going to have. Qayaq was ordered by his father-in-law to go and get it. He wanted it killed so he could feed the village with ptarmigan meat.

Qayaq went out early in the morning to look for the bird. He was told what direction to take by his father-in-law. When he saw the big white bird, it was in the distance but it was so very large that it looked like a mountain of snow. When the bird saw Qayaq coming, it sped toward him. When Qayaq saw this, he ran fearlessly to meet it. When the bird came upon Qayaq, it exhaled and fire shot out of its mouth and nostrils. This singed Qayaq. His hair was burnt and also his eyebrows. But he did not withdraw. He fought with the ptarmigan for several days. At the end of this fight, the ptarmigan was dead. This ptarmigan was not used for the great feast.

When Qayaq reached home, people were already feasting and dancing. They believed that Qayaq had died. Instead Qayaq had killed the bird. Their assumption made Qayaq angry, but he did not do anything. He did his best to be good to the people that took him in, and he had a wife who was one of them. Here also were his children.

When the summer came, people were hunting on the sea. One day Qayaq was on the sea in his huge kayak catching sea animals. While he was not too far from the shore, a big wind came. This sudden squall almost capsized his kayak. Just an instant before the sea had been calm, and now this terrible storm engulfed him. All around and close to him the sea looked calm, but these huge waves were giving him and his kayak a terrible time. He knew if he did not do something, he was going to drown.

In his desperation, he remembered the pebbles that his father had made him swallow. He made a gurgling noise, and one of them came up to his mouth. He spit the pebble out in the direction from which the wind was coming. He was now on a calm sea. The storm suddenly abated; this made him feel that he was going to continue living. He paddled for home, and as he was coming close to the shore, he saw someone lying on the beach.

After beaching his kayak, he went up to the man on the ground. This man was dead. He recognized him as the village Umialik, the chief, his father-in-law. His father-in-law had been blowing wind through his sleeve. He had pulled his hood on and over his face, then with his mouth next to his armpit he blew through his sleeve. This made a great storm for Qayaq while he was out on the sea where he was hunting. Right on the bridge of the Umialik's nose between his eyes, there, embedded in his flesh, was the pebble Qayaq had spit out against the big wind. This pebble had killed the Umialik.

Many times when he had fought to save people, he had not killed any one of his in-laws. This was the only one Qayaq had killed with no intention to do so, the Umialik of this village.

It is said here that Qayaq gave many children to his wife. But soon the old longing for adventure came over him again, and he went on down along the coast.

Qayaq walked and walked.

He came upon Tlinget people that had totem poles. From a distance he watched one huge village, with a huge structure in the middle and totem poles all around. In this village lived a beautiful princess. Qayaq watched her as she went in and out of her dwelling. He noticed that she caught birds by snaring them. She took these into her home, plucked the feathers and cooked them for food.

One day Qayaq turned himself into a little hawk and sat on top of a totem pole. He sat there many days before the princess noticed he was sitting there. When Qayaq noticed that the princess saw him, he flew away.

The princess set a snare on top of the totem pole. Qayaq flew to the snare, and he was caught. Qayaq's feathers were plucked and he was cooked. All his bones were clean, all the meat was eaten. But even now, when he was nothing but dry bones, Qayaq still could think. He thought to himself, "I want her to gather my bones together and take me out." The beautiful princess picked up the front of her skirt to form a pouch, gathered these bones together and took them out to where she usually dumped bird bones. When she did so, Qayaq became a man. He became her husband.

Many storytellers always say that Qayaq had children at the mouth of Selawik River, at the mouth of Yukon River, and some were born down in southeast Alaska among the Tlinget people.

Qayaq took the form of animals many times and the form of other human beings many times, always doing good against evil.

He was known to have travelled all over what is now known as Alaska; also to have gone over to what is now known as Canada. Many storytellers, even today, would say, "Qayaq was on this river." Many a storyteller can say, "Qayaq belonged to us, travelled on

QAYAQ VISITS THE HEADWATERS OF THE SELAWIK RIVER AND EVENTUALLY FINDS HIS WAY HOME

Kilalogak (Whales)
Mona Ohoveluk

our river." But he was the twelfth son of a couple that lived at the mouth of the Selawik River. This couple were great, huge human beings.

Selawik Lake at that time was very deep. Whales went into this lake. It is, today, thirty miles long and thirty miles wide. In order to get to Selawik Lake, there is another lake that is fresh water that is Kobuk Lake. This lake is forty miles long, ten to twenty miles wide in places. These lakes are near Kotzebue which is known to be an ancient trading centre. These two lakes were deep at that time, and many whales went into them.

Qayaq's parents who had lived at the mouth of Selawik River caught whales, and the bones of these animals were many. Today, the mouth of Selawik River still carries the name Sauniqtuk, which means, "Place of bones."

This couple were parents of twelve sons. When each one became a man, he was powerful and capable of doing many great feats. Each one left the parents in a kayak paddling away, following the Selawik River to the east. Qayaq being their twelfth and the youngest son heard these words as he was growing up, "*Qayaqtuagaqniqtuq*" (Forever-riding-a-kayak). Each son had left them, always paddling toward the east in a kayak.

But Qayaq's father understood that there was an unseen force that influenced each and every one of his sons, that made them leave to help the weak against many wild animals, birds, and evil human beings.

Nevertheless the parents grieved over their sons that did not return. When Qayaq was leaving he promised them that he was going to come back to be with them again. Even though he had travelled all over, he always had it in his mind that he was going to return to be with them.

Qayaq walked and walked.

    Qayaq walked to the head of Selawik River. He
went to a place where he had left his skin kayak. It
was made with a wood frame and covered with seal-
skins. A long time had passed, and when he touched
his kayak, it crumbled. He tried to make use of it but
it was rotten. This grieved him. He did not know
what to do. He put down his bedding and sat down,
feeling very sad. He had to do something. Looking
around him, he noticed there were birch trees,
spruce trees and water willows. Along the banks of
the river there were long underground root-like vines
hanging over the bank that had been exposed by
erosions. He knew these could be materials to make
some kind of craft. What kind of craft he did not know.

    "I will gather birchbark to cover the frame. It is
smooth and hard and could be used to protect me
from water." He gathered this and laid it in a pile. He cut down
birch trees for the frame and paddle. He gathered vine-like roots
from the bank of the river. These roots were pliant and very
strong, and could be used to lash the materials together. (This
fibrous material is called *mamaaq*.) He went through the forest of
spruce trees to gather pitch that was plentiful. This substance is
yellow and sticky before it is exposed to the air too long. He had
enough materials for a good-sized craft.

    As loud as he could he said: "I have overcome evil with good in
my many travels. There were animals, birds and evil human beings.
My power came from something great. Or someone has helped me.
If there is someone who has helped me, I need help now. There is

Man Singing
with Arms Uplifted
Levi Tetpon

Joyful Young Man
Kingmeata Etidlooie

a greater force than I know, I need help now." He shouted to the west wind, to the east wind, to the south wind, and to the north wind. With a big voice, he shouted. His voice echoed all around him.

After he did this, he went into his tent and fell asleep. Sometime during the night, he could hear voices and he peeked out and there in front of him was a frame of a large canoe. There was much business in the air and there was much noise from laughter. This laughter came from animals gathered to help him. There were a pair of beavers now fashioning a double-bladed paddle. They made much noise as they gnawed on a birch tree. There were a pair of porcupines, their cheeks bulging with pitch ready to seal the canoe so it would not leak. They were squealing with laughter. Two large cranes were busy lashing the birch bark in place using the long, smooth, already split and cleaned underground roots. With its sharp beak one of them made holes and wove the gunwale all around the canoe, the other doing the same from the opposite side of the canoe. Qayaq could hear the noise the cranes made as they worked. They were noisy as they made holes and wove the roots through them: "*Tattuuk, tattuuk.*" Qayaq did not disturb the busy animals and two birds. He lay back on his bedding and fell asleep again.

The sun was warm already when Qayaq woke up again. There was no more noise. The canoe was ready. It was beautiful. He took it to the edge of the river and launched it. He piled all his belongings in it and paddled down Selawik River.

Qayaq paddled and paddled.

When he reached the mouth of Selawik River nothing was

there except a pile of bones. Qayaq examined the
ground where his parents' large home had stood.
Where the home had been there was a short stump
sticking out of the ground. The house had wasted
away, a mighty tree had grown in its place, and now
only that tree's stump was left. Where was his parents' huge house? Where were they? From the way
things looked here, hundreds of years had gone by.
He was filled with grief.

From then on, people saw a little hawk sitting on
this stump, grieving. The hawk's head was bent down,
its little beak laid on its breast in a sign of much
grief. Qayaq had not fulfilled his promise of seeing
his parents again. His grief was so very great that he
turned himself into a little hawk. Many years hence
this little hawk was still seen sitting on the stump.

In the water in front of where their house had
been was a huge canoe laden with implements that Qayaq had gathered in his travels. People copied these implements. They copied
this canoe to make their own birchbark canoes. When they no
longer used birchbark for canoes, they still used it to make berry
buckets and water buckets. These were fashioned and lashed with
strong underground roots woven on their rims. The weaving on
the buckets was done like the lashing of roots that the two cranes
had woven on the gunwales of Qayaq's canoe.

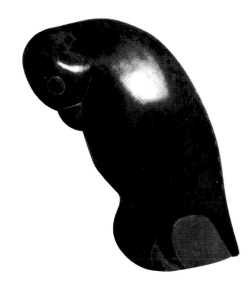

Hawk with Bowed Head
Eliasie Weetaluktuk

The story of Qayaq is the oldest story ever told by the Inupiat. It is the story of the family that long ago lived at the mouth of Selawik River.

Many years ago during the winter, during the stormiest, coldest, and shortest days of the winter, an expert storyteller was chosen to tell it. The storyteller stayed quiet just long enough to eat and to sleep. This story is so very long that it always took a storyteller one moon to tell it. People watched for the new moon and when the very first crescent showed, the storyteller began.

Today, people are trying to bring back the telling of the many episodes of this long story. I listened to one storyteller on the radio; it took him less than thirty minutes to tell the whole tale.

As many years went by, The Epic of Qayaq *was passed on from generation to generation orally. Not written, parts of the tale were dropped and others added, but we know every tribe among the Eskimo have it. Every tribe believes that it came from their own river. They say, "Qayaqtuagaqniqtuq (Forever-riding-a-kayak) came from our river."*

But I know it came from my river, Selawik River.

Akkumii (THE END)

LELA KIANA OMAN

LIST OF PLATES

KENOJUAK ASHEVAK B. 1927   47
[Aoudla Pudlat]
CAPE DORSET
Spirits at Night, 1989
lithograph 8/50
40.5 x 45.5

THOMAS SIVURAQ B. 1941   49
BAKER LAKE
Big Man, 1979
black stone
20 x 18 x 23

JOANASI NALUIYUK B. 1917   50
SALLUIT
*Shaman with Bear
on Head*, 1980
grey stone
17.5 x 10 x 13

MARION TUU'LUUQ B. 1910   60
[Nugyugulik Tudluk]
BAKER LAKE
*Animals Disguising
as People*, 1975
stonecut; stencil 44/50
63.7 x 94.8

MALAYA AKULUKJUK B. 1915   67
[Leesee Kakee]
PANGNIRTUNG
Sunrise at Tanaqaaq
tapestry 15/20
104 x 136

GEELA AKULUKJUK B. 1952   69
[Enukee Akulukjuk]
PANGNIRTUNG
Sudden Movement, 1985
stencil 21/50
39.3 x 34.8

HELEN KALVAK (1901 - 1984)   70
[Ida Aivek]
HOLMAN ISLAND
Running Caribou, 1980
stencil 42/50
50.75 x 62.5

EEGEEVUDLUK RAGEE   82
(1920 - 1983)
CAPE DORSET
Drum Dancer, 1978
stonecut; stencil 44/50
51.3 x 45.8

PITSEOLAK NIVIAQSI B. 1947   89
CAPE DORSET
Kuuqapik (The River), 1992
lithograph 21/50
66.5 x 51

JESSIE OONARK (1906 - 1985)   98
[Phillipa Iksiraq]
BAKER LAKE
Angutkoq, 1975
serigraph 34/50
33 x 40.7

KANAYUK TUKALAK B. 1937   100
POVUNGNITUK
Untitled [Weasel] 1961
stencil 17/50
46 x 61

ANDREW KARPIK B. 1964   108
PANGNIRTUNG
Char Fishing, 1986
etching 2/50
56.7 x 38

MYRA KUKIIYAUT B. 1929   109
BAKER LAKE
*The Shaman Becomes
a Wolf*, 1980
stencil 12/50
56.5 x 76.3

LUKASSIE TUKALAK B. 1917   112
[Caroline Qumaluk]
POVUNGNITUK
*The 'Evil Spirit' Expects to Devour
the Man*, 1987
stonecut 3/50
42 x 60

MONA OHOVELUK B. 1935   116
HOLMAN ISLAND
Kilalogak (Whales), 1978
stonecut 27/50
50.9 x 76

LEVI TETPON   117
ELIM, ALASKA
*Man Singing with
Arms Uplifted*
brown soapstone
18 x 17.5 x 8

KINGMEATA ETIDLOOIE   118
(1915 - 1989)
CAPE DORSET
Joyful Young Man, 1981
stonecut; stencil 16/50
61.4 x 81.8

ELIASIE WEETALUKTUK B. 1949   119
INOUCDJOUAC
Hawk with Bowed Head, 1974
grey stone
16 x 11 x 15